SUBSIDIA BIBLICA

34

JOHN KILGALLEN, S.J.

A WEALTH OF REVELATION

The Four Evangelists' Introduction to Their Gospels

EDITRICE PONTIFICIO ISTITUTO BIBLICO

© 2009 Editrice Pontificio Istituto Biblico
Piazza della Pilotta, 35 - 00187 Roma
tel. 06 6781567 - fax 06 6780588

ISBN 978-88-7653-640-3

PREFACE

Around 33 AD the public life of Jesus, for many months highly contested, ended in ignominy and crucifixion—a terrible tragedy in the eyes of many who, at one time or another, judged him to be good and powerful and wise. Believers in Jesus, those who at last saw him raised from the dead and those who believed thereafter in Jesus risen, began and went on for decades to tell the stories they knew about Jesus and the aftermath of his departure from this life (e.g., Pentecost). They did this for at least four reasons: to move non-believers to faith in Jesus, to defend Christian faith against a variety of attacks, to instruct those seeking baptism in the beliefs of Christianity and the moral teaching of Jesus and to provide homily material for weekly Christian gatherings, similar to our Sunday homilies today.

Eventually, certain Christians thought it most helpful to their fellow Christians to gather certain of these many stories, whether of what Jesus did or said, or what had happened to him, and present them in the form of a biography of Jesus. What moved each of them to present the story of Jesus were the needs of his audience. Often, these first-century Christian groups suffered opposition and even actual persecution. Such situations, and others, motivated gospel writers to offer consolation and encouragement through a telling of the Jesus story. The needs of the audiences determined, in the minds of the evangelists, just what materials they should present and suggest just how to present these materials. We recall that the original audiences of our gospels had already, before the gospels had been sent to them, been introduced to Jesus by missionaries and preachers of the word, and believed in him. What prompted stories, then, about Jesus was not an unbelieving community, but one which needed to hear a telling of Jesus' life that would help them understand God's plan in Jesus better, live their commitment to Jesus Christ more perfectly and sustain persecution. Each author looked to the audience of his time, to its needs, and then constructed his version of the Jesus story that would be most helpful to his readers. Who would not be inspired by hearing the Master speak and watching his many wonders take place, watching, too, how he died and what his resurrection implied?

Diversity and Freedom
The four gospels are, then, attempts to present the person of Jesus in such a way that their readers can see clearly the meaning of Jesus for their particu-

lar moment and understand the implications of their following Jesus. But, as one might expect, as audiences differed in their needs, so gospel renditions of Jesus differed among themselves. Each gospel pursues its goal in its own way; indeed, the four gospels are recognizably quite different in their telling. Let us think more about this diversity.

First, each author, while in possession of many of the same facts and words and deeds of Jesus' life, had his own perception of Jesus to communicate, a perception that would, as we have already emphasized, help their readers in their Christian lives. This does not mean that the four contradict one another, for they all believe that Jesus is divine savior of the world and its judge; it only means that each writer, for the particular needs of his readers, chose to present Jesus in his particular way. Thus, diversity exists without detracting at all from the essential unity that is the person, Jesus Christ.

Second, let us be more specific and reflective about our statement that each evangelist is guided by what we call "the needs" of the Christian people to whom each writer is writing. Scholarship generally affirms that Mark's audience, about 65–70 AD, suffered in Rome from Imperial Roman opposition and even persecution; certainly, Christianity was against Roman Law, which essentially recognized and promoted only the Roman religion and tolerated no other; the young audience needed help in understanding the meaning of Jesus in that perilous and threatening time. At other moments and elsewhere in the Mediterranean basin, Matthew in 85 AD and John in 90–95 AD wrote the story of Jesus in such wise as to show Jewish Christians that Jewish non-Christian opponents were terribly wrong in their denial of Jesus and their persecutions of his followers. Luke, in 85 AD, does not write to Christian believers because they are persecuted (though he certainly alerts them to the possibility), but to Gentile Christians who, Luke thinks, should clearly understand the universal divine plan of salvation and their place in it; this includes the moral perfection of the reader who believes in Jesus. That is, each writer thinks that his readers will be best served by looking at Jesus in a way that addresses their needs, their problems, their questions, their concerns. The assumption, of course, is that the needs, etc. of each audience will be in large measure different in each case and so the gospel responses will be different. And, of course, it means that the gospels will above all be "first-century documents". We can safely say that without realizing/learning the influence of the needs of Christian communities on the evangelists, one will not fully understand why the gospels offer different versions of the life of Jesus.

It follows then that the gospel biographies of Jesus are not an attempt by any of our four evangelists simply to write history; these writers want to deepen what has already been believed. Historical facts are essential to deeper belief, for the human being needs as much conviction as his intelligence demands in order to sustain the leap to faith. But our writers, rather than being concerned solely with history, rather use historical details in the service of securing and deepening the faith of those to whom they write.

Third, together with the particular concern driving each gospel, is the freedom of each writer to pursue his goal as he sees fit. If we understand the reality of this freedom we will better adjust to the fact that, e.g., Mark has no sermon on the mount or that John is not concerned with Jesus' moral teachings or that Luke felt obliged to write two volumes and not one, as did Matthew, Mark and John. Indeed, to underestimate the freedom of each of God's literary writers is to create obstacles and contradictions within the gospels that can only harm the values the gospels mean to offer. Each writer must be understood to be absolutely free in choosing his materials and his manner of telling, organizing and adjusting these materials about Jesus. It is true that God is the author of every gospel, indeed its principal author; but to affirm this is not to deny at all the freedom of the human author to choose his materials, his methods and his goals as he thinks best. One thinks best when one affirms that God uses the freedom (and talents) of the human author in such wise as to produce both what he and she want as believing first-century Christians.

The Writer's Choice

Each gospel begins Jesus' public life with the same elements: the public preaching of John the Baptist in regard to Jesus and the anointing of Jesus by the Holy Spirit at his baptism (and his being tempted in the desert for forty days). From that anointing begins a new kind of life for Jesus, one very much different from his first thirty years of life and one which reveals who he really is and, indeed, the purpose of his being. Yet, it is clear that no gospel begins its story with these two elements. Each gospel writer has introduced the public life of Jesus with other material than that which belongs to the public life, a different material recognizable as an introduction, or a type thereof; again, as the diversity of the introductions indicates, each writer chose what he thought would be an excellent way of introducing the public-life figure of Jesus.

Just to present the public life of Jesus from his anointing onward apparently will not reveal sufficiently the deepest meaning of Jesus. Each writer thought that if he could only add an introduction, one he saw as fitting, to the public life of Jesus, then his audience would have the best chance to understand who the adult Jesus really is for their particular lives.

Uniqueness of Introductions

Indeed, we do not have to suppose that a gospel must have an introduction, or each its own; it is from our reading that we know that gospels have introductions, and that no evangelist's introduction is the same as anyone else's. But, in harmony with the rest of the gospel, each introduction presents, though in anticipatory form, the central lessons which the author has in mind for his audience. Thus, each introduction is tailor-made for each of the four presentations of the figure of Jesus. As noted earlier, since each gospel is written to its own audience, at its own location and time, and for its own purpose, it seems only right to expect each evangelist to present what he thinks will introduce best his particular telling of the Jesus story. It is a question of means to end; that is, the writer will choose his introduction material to fit his goal in telling about the public life of Jesus. It follows then that it would be for us a significant error to use, for instance, Matthew's introduction as an introduction to Luke's story. Each introduction is written to fit its own gospel.

Necessity of Introductions

A final thought is in order, one regarding the nature of an introduction. An introduction contains in it what the author wants the reader to take with him throughout the rest of the book. From this fact we can say that each author has constructed his introduction with material or affirmations about Jesus that the reader never forgets, but takes with him and uses as a guide to understand the rest of the book that follows. Indeed, some things in the introduction may not be repeated again (e.g., the all-important testimony to announcements about the virginal conception of Jesus and his divinity, or the description of Jesus as the Word-made-flesh), but each of these announcements should always be remembered and thus should guide the reading of the story that each introduces. As one can see from literature in general, the introduction is very important; indeed, that it exists at all is its own testimony to its importance for achieving what the author wants to achieve. It seems, then, very reasonable that we look to the introduction of each gospel in order to find out what each writer wants the reader to take with him as he begins to read the writer's story of the adult life of Jesus. It seems good to study these introductions in a thorough manner, to enjoy and use the wealth of their contributions to understanding the public life of Jesus.

We will do well, then, to concentrate now on what each gospel writer wants to say in preparation for reading the wonderful, the tragic, the glorious life of Jesus. The better we understand the introductions, the better we will understand the adult Jesus, object of our faith. To offer some evidence of the influence of the introductions in their respective gospels, we shall briefly discuss the different versions of the public life of Jesus in the light of each of the introductions.

TABLE OF CONTENTS

Introduction

We know from what we write ourselves, and from reading the works of others, how important an introduction to a book is. An introduction usually offers readers the right understanding by which to enter a story, and directions the author wants them to follow in their subsequent reading; often, too, the introduction presents the themes to be developed or to be given meaning in the body of the work. Again, like an overture in music, the introduction presents the major ideas that will permeate the writing. All writers want their readers to understand well their introductions and to keep in mind what they offer as guides to the ideas and moods and images in which their readers will be immersed as they pass through the rest of what has been written.

Variety
Each of the gospels has its introduction, its affirmation(s) to be developed. Perhaps unexpectedly, the gospels differ significantly their introductory presentations: Mark has an introduction of just half a verse; Matthew has an introduction of two chapters that consists basically of three stories; Luke, too, has an introduction of two chapters, but it is made up of seven stories, accompanied by summaries; finally, John introduces his gospel with a poem eighteen verses in length. Immediately we face the reality that each gospel writer uses his authorial freedom to introduce his story as he thinks best.

Guided by the evangelist's personal choice, we look to see how each introduction will prepare us for, and lead us into, its gospel's main story. We seek to understand what we are to learn from the introduction that will help us grasp most fully the meaning of this particular gospel's central narrative about the public life of Jesus. Indeed, acknowledgement of the uniqueness of each gospel introduction makes us anticipate an overall unique gospel narrative. A successful study of the four gospel introductions will assure us of the guiding thoughts with which each evangelist intends to lead us through his particularized presentation of the life of the adult Jesus, including his preaching, death and resurrection.

Identifying Gospel Introductions

The passages which I have I have identified as introductions—Mark, 1, 1; Matthew 1 and 2; Luke 1 and 2, John 1, 1-18—can be challenged on the grounds that they are not formally introductions. For instance, there is a period in all four gospels in which John the Baptist, the adult, is presented, with his preaching and witnessing to "someone greater". Indeed, many like to think of the story of John as an introduction to or preparation for the Jesus story—introduction, in the sense that John is certainly not the main character in the gospels and disappears rather quickly from the gospel stories. Then, too, in the synoptic gospels, this presentation of John the Baptist is followed by the baptism of Jesus and, in three gospels, his period of temptations in the desert; since these earliest stories of Jesus seem to be a preparation for his public preaching and deeds, many think of them too as part of the introduction to the life of Jesus. The "introductory" story of the adult John, in John's gospel, is followed by Jesus' choosing of certain disciples; some scholars have the impression that this period of calling disciples is a preparation for the upcoming wandering of Jesus with these disciples that characterizes Jesus' preaching life. All of this material, which antecedes Jesus' stepping, as it were, onto the public stage of words and deeds and challenges—is it not better to say that all the matter which precedes Jesus' public life should be considered as part of the introductions to Jesus?

Criteria for Identifying Introductions

While a case can be made for calling all that which precedes Jesus' public life an "introduction", there still is a valid distinction between what begins each gospel as a defining statement or series of statements about the Jesus soon to be described and those other, later stories about the adult Jesus that precede or lead into his public life. Certainly Matthew and Luke, following classical styles, tell us what the childhood of Jesus reveals about him; in these stories Jesus does nothing or little, and they look forward to guide the reader's understanding of the adult Jesus. John begins with a poem about the Word, a term never seen again in the gospel, but very useful and forceful for beginning it. Mark has only half a verse before bringing John the adult to us, but it is a verse which defines Jesus as no later story in his gospel can. These statements are our concern in this book. It is to these four "Jesus-introductions" we now turn our attention. It is in them that the hand of the evangelist is most visible, as is his will to reveal, as fully as he can, the meaning of the "public" Jesus who will be the central aspect of his gospel.

Difficulties in Presenting the Meaning of Jesus

A peculiarity about the gospels follows logically from these four introductions. These latter argue that the evangelists are convinced they will never bring out the deepest meaning of Jesus simply by telling stories about his public life and death. In his own lifetime, Jesus was never understood fully by any human being. Paul is witness to this: he preaches Jesus crucified and risen, for only in the death and resurrection does Paul think it possible to reveal who Jesus is for us all. One finds very little of the pre-crucifixion life of Jesus in Paul; "trust in and learn from the meaning of his death and resurrection" is his message. The evangelists are different from Paul; not denying the value of Jesus' death and resurrection, they mean to draw out as much meaning from Jesus' public life as they can. And with the study each gospel writer knew that if he was to succeed in giving his audience a profound understanding of the "crucified and risen" Jesus, he would have to introduce his story with very clear expressions about Jesus, expressions of each evangelist guided by the faith lived from Jesus' resurrection to the time of their writing their gospels. The introductions to the gospels serve most of all to make clear who the Jesus is who will live his adult, public life; and so the reader can understand from the beginning of his reading, by virtue of these introductions, what the contemporaries of Jesus might have at best only suspected him to be. In this regard Saint Paul's question is pertinent, "Would they have crucified the Lord of glory, if they had known who he really was?" No, and, it is to be noted explicitly, not even Jesus' friends at the time understood him sufficiently. Because the adult life of Jesus is so perplexing, it is the particular function of each introduction to convey the most significant or profound meaning of Jesus to the audience, and thereby to teach the reader how to interpret the adult Jesus adequately, no matter what he is doing or saying at any particular moment, and no matter what people are thinking and saying about him at the moment. It is this understanding which will best serve to answer problems of the writer's readers.

Jesus on Jesus and Our Reaction

Before discussing the introductions it would be good to reflect for a moment on what the adult Jesus said about himself to his contemporaries about the purpose of his life. It makes sense to begin, even though briefly, with Jesus' own words and deeds about himself, to look to his own self-revelation, if we want to enter into a study about his meaning. Yet, even though Jesus' self-revelation about his purpose can help the reader understand him better, the people of his time never perceived from this self-revelation the fullness of his meaning. Again, the existence of the introductions from the four authors is their own proof that even what Jesus does and says about himself needs sharpening and further profundity. The introductions provide this fuller clarity.

What was the purpose of Jesus' public life in his own words? Looking to the synoptic gospels, we can say that Jesus affirms that he was sent by God to announce the joyful news of the nearness of the kingdom of God (e.g., Luke 4, 43: "It is necessary that I announce the joyful kingdom of God"). The kingdom of God is a metaphor, indicating that all the blessings, all the happiness, the fulfillment of all hopes, one's being one's best self perfectly—all of this will happen because God is king. As king God through love will bring completion and perfection to everyone. The news is, in part, joyful because it says that the kingdom has begun with Jesus' presence, and because Jesus shows the way into the full, complete kingdom, whenever it comes. After his public life, Jesus will provide the Spirit which will strengthen the believer to make the choices to enter that kingdom. Indeed, the dynamic, perfecting presence of God the Son and God the Spirit suggest that the rule of God has already begun: "The kingdom of God is within (i.e., among) you".

A subordinate but essential purpose of Jesus' public life is this: he was sent by God to call sinners to leave sin and take on a new life (Luke 5, 32: "I have come to call sinners to repentance"). This purpose is a subordinate purpose because repentance is a means to an end, the end of entering into the fullness of the kingdom of God that Jesus announces. Thus, Jesus announces the beginning of the kingdom, calls us to prepare ourselves to enter it, and instructs us on how to make this preparation.

If we look at the fourth gospel, Jesus says something very similar to what the synoptics report, though in language particular to John. Simply put, Jesus assures all that "he has come that they may have life and have it to the full" (10, 10). This is not "kingdom" language, but it clearly fits in with that language. Indeed, John's own purpose in writing is that "you may believe that Jesus is the Messiah, Son of God, and thereby have life without end" (20, 31). This belief will entail, in its own way, a change called conversion.

The Teaching of Jesus as a Problem

Jesus was rather abruptly put to death by being crucified. The reason for this was not his miracles or his own piety or lack thereof; the reason was that he taught, directly or indirectly, a way into the kingdom which differed notably from what many of the religious teachers of his locality taught. Thus, he not only asked for repentance but also taught repeatedly and in no uncertain terms what repentance concretely means. Many leaders of Jesus' time grew in dissatisfaction with him, dissatisfaction to the point of anger. One can point out less noble motives for this opposition to Jesus (e.g., jealousy), but there is always in the Israel of his time a worry or anxiety that goes beyond personal enmity or jealousy. Israel had learned, from two terrible exiles (721 BC and 587 BC), just how angry and punitive God can be with those who disobey his teaching. As a corollary, anyone who now presented himself as a teacher who contradicted or eliminated all or part of the Mosaic Law or its traditions as understood by the ruling teachers threatened to bring about again the horrors of the past. This person must be removed. Jesus, the false teacher, could not be allowed to teach. Either he had to give up his teaching or he had to die. The latter proved to be the case.

The Identity of Jesus as Question

Jesus' teaching proved attractive to many people in Israel for it was a teaching which seemed to them to be a correct understanding of God's will and the Mosaic Law. But Jesus' life did not last long. Ultimately, the question which had been asked in his public life became the final question when he was on the cross: who was he? Many had guessed that he was a prophet, a rather general appraisal meaning that he "spoke on behalf of God". More particularly, various people suggested that Jesus was the prophet whom God had promised to Moses as Moses' successor in leading Israel (cf. Deuteronomy 15, 15.18). Some suggested that, with his miracles and call for repentance, he was Elijah, who preached repentance

and was involved in miracles (e.g., I Kings 17, 9-24) and has finally come
to prepare the people for the final judgment (cf. the prophecy of Malachi
3, 23). A few concluded that he was the Messiah, that longed-for king
who would finally establish a kingdom in which all Israelites, and every
Israelite, would enjoy forever the greatest of God's blessings to the full.
None of these interpretations of Jesus won the day in his public life; and
his death upset everyone's previous judgment about him. All the more
mysterious is his person when one thinks of his resurrection from the
dead. This is not a resurrection like those believed in by many Jews of
this generation: they understood that the resurrection from the dead would
take place at the end of time. Jesus rose from the dead immediately after
his death, a bizarre and totally unexpected, unheard of event. Who is he?

The Identity of Jesus as Answer
While many of his followers kept alive in various preachings and in
various accounts the things he said and did and was in his public life, the
first authentic rendition we have of this life and its meaning is Mark's
gospel, some forty years after Jesus' death (c. 70 AD). Matthew and
Luke, basing themselves heavily on Mark, wrote their stories about 85
AD and John about 95 AD. Each of these gospels is aimed at a particular
audience (which, we must remember, is not us) and the story of Jesus is
told in order to help the audiences in whatever the authors felt they needed help. In short, Mark could help his Christians in Rome to put up with,
or at least to understand, persecution if he told the story of Jesus in a way
that would accomplish that purpose. Luke could help his Christians by
giving them a life of Jesus told in such a way that they would know how
reliable were the things they had been taught. Matthew and John wrote
their gospels, too, for specific circumstances and needs, particularly to
strengthen Christian's faithful adherence to Jesus in times of opposition.
But every one of them felt that he had to somehow make clear in his stories what would make up for the lack of clarity about Jesus in his public
appearances. That is, if in his life Jesus remained a mystery, and later just
a recounting of facts about the public life was, though good, not sufficient
to reveal the deepest meaning of his being, was there a way to make clear
to the reader of the gospel who Jesus really is, without distorting the facts
of his public life?

The answer of each evangelist included the writing of an introduction to his gospel. An introduction gives a writer the opportunity to define Jesus profoundly and to present ideas about him which reach to the furthest end of the author's writing. He need not repeat those ideas throughout his writing, because the very nature of an introduction assures him that those ideas are available to an intelligent reader throughout the gospel. Matthew, Mark, Luke and John have presented their readers with introductions, each in his own way and style. They ask the reader to take very seriously these introductory statements and stories, and to bring them to whatever part of the public life of Jesus they are reading. Thus, in a gospel where almost everyone is trying to guess Jesus' true meaning and many fail miserably to do so, the reader knows from the beginning (specifically from the introduction), who Jesus is. As a result the reader of a gospel is often drawn into feeling at one with those who are trying to understand Jesus, but all the while understanding Jesus because of the gospel's introduction. It is this knowledge of who Jesus is that enables the reader to have, among other things, the right interpretation of Jesus' death, an interpretation that is escaping those being portrayed.

The Time Gap
We cannot overemphasize the importance of recognizing what it means to write a story some 40 years or more after the events it describes. We need only imagine our writing in 2040 about something that happened in 2000. By 2040 how much reflection would have gone into appreciating what had happened 40 years before! Nor do we wish to underestimate what it means to say that Matthew and Luke, though they did not know each other, did know and use Mark's gospel—while at the same time deciding, each for his own purposes, that they needed new stories, added to and beyond Mark, about Jesus. Scholars suggest that John might have used a source Luke knew, but find no source shared with Mark or Matthew.

Summary
In summary, we note (not for the first time!) that to tell the story of Jesus properly—what he taught and did and the injustice of his death and the justness of his rising from the dead—one needs an introduction. An intro-duction offers a clarity which arises from more than just a repetition of

stories about the public life of Jesus will not provide. On the contrary, the stories about the public life of Jesus are made clearer by the introductions which lead us into them. Without the introductions we suffer in our understanding of how God intervened through Jesus in our world. With the introductions evangelists are able to express what was the meaning of Jesus for their audiences. Here we find the best expressions of these four believers in Jesus, as they handed on their faith to strengthen the faith of other Christians.

Let us then consider the introductions to the four gospels. We could have used the temporal sequence to line up our gospels for us: Mark (70 AD), Matthew and Luke (85 AD), John (95 AD). But given the various lengths of the four Introductions, we begin first with Mark (the shortest of the introductions), then go on to John, and end with Matthew and Luke (the longest).

Before one works through each of the sections below one should read carefully the verses and chapters we identify as the introduction to the gospel. In this way, we avoid excessive quotation, and give ourselves the best chance to reach the goal of our study: to understand not so much what is written in the present book, but above all what is written in the gospels themselves.

Mark

After noting in the introduction of this book that each gospel has an introduction, it is surprising to note that Mark offers his reader as introduction an incomplete sentence: "The beginning of the good news of Jesus, Christ and Son of God". One might pass over this verse, considering it merely to be a note from the evangelist that his gospel begins at this point: "Start reading here".

But then a second thought occurs. Not only, the theory goes, should one "start here", but Mark wanted to make sure that the reader knew the point of view he was taking with regard to Jesus Christ, the well-known person about whom he was writing. But could there possibly be confusion on this latter point? In a certain sense, at this initial point of the gospel, yes; since Mark immediately launches into a description of John the Baptist, perhaps Mark thought he should signal, through these first words, that the story he tells is about Jesus, not about John. As will immediately become clear, Jesus will be the main character in Mark's story, and so John the Baptist, though occurring first in the story Mark is about to tell, will, literally speaking, be reduced in importance and will become a preparation for Jesus.

But another, more tantalizing, suggestion is that the word "beginning" means that the entire story of Jesus, from baptism to resurrection, is just the beginning of the plan of God that will continue through all times and places. What began with the earthly life of Jesus continues in his community even now and to the end of time. Jesus' public life is only the beginning. In this view, the entire Gospel is a story only about the human life which is the "beginning".

The Key Issue
But whatever one decides about the meaning of "beginning" in this verse, it is not the key issue in Mark's first words. The key issue is found in the two titles given Jesus. They constitute the introduction's most important element. Messiah and Son of God are titles which the entire gospel is going to explain for the benefit of its readers.

It is worth noting that these two titles in the gospel's first and verbless sentence are not "story-telling" as is the rest of the gospel. They stand out as the author's affirmation, Mark's faith-statement. They are titles which the rest of the gospel will explain.

"Good News"

As the for the term "good news" (usually found as "gospel"), Mark's use of "good" is reassuring. It stands in apparent contrast to the story about Jesus which follows, a story full of puzzles, challenges and opposition which ends in the humiliating and "untimely" death of Jesus. By using the term "good news" in his introduction, Mark makes us aware that everything in his story is ultimately good. But in itself it does not specify, as used in the introduction, just how the "good news" of Jesus is good.

Even the name "Jesus" in Mark's introduction does not reveal much. In itself the name means "God saves through the one bearing this name". The name is thus suggestive, especially in the context of what Mark and his Christian readers already believe about Jesus. But the introduction tells us that Jesus is going to be looked on from the standpoint of the titles "Messiah" and "Son of God", not savior. The name "Jesus" in Mark's gospel is thus to be taken as referring to the person whom people touched, heard, addressed, and watched. He is the person about whom people argued—and differed in their interpretations in the 30s AD. And it is this person who Mark feels must be explained under these two titles to his audience in 65-70 AD.

Central Titles of Jesus as Aids to Readers

When we come, then, to the final two nouns of Mark's first verse, we have not just the naming of the story's hero, but the central interpretation of him which will be used in the gospel. Jesus is the Messiah and Jesus is Son of God. These are two faith statements, two ways of understanding Jesus. (By the time of Mark's gospel, Jesus was known as "Jesus Christ", but Mark separates "Christ" from "Jesus" to emphasize the functional role of Messiah.) Both titles are to serve as guides during our reading from the moment we begin the first gospel page. By meeting Jesus this way, the reader is always to remember that at every juncture of the Marcan gospel he is reading about the Messiah and the Son of God. True, Jesus will make people think of himself under many other interpretations, for example (and perhaps most of all) Son of Man and prophet. But, given the prominence of this verse as the head of the gospel, and the very purpose of an introduction, Mark wants his reader to know from the beginning that Jesus, now and throughout this gospel, is Messiah and Son of God.

The Christian Audience of Mark

Before beginning a more thorough discussion of the titles "Messiah" and "Son of God", it is important to make explicit that the audience of Mark's gospel are Christians who come from in and around Rome. They already believe—as their baptism shows—that Jesus is Messiah and Son of God. Since their baptism they have been called to be faithful to what God has destined for them, even, as now, persecution. We can note here that Paul, in the mid-fifties AD, reminded the Corinthian community (I Corinthians 1, 13) that Christ, and no one else, is the one who died for them, that in no other name than Christ's were they baptized. Against this background Mark's group, some twenty years later, can surely be presumed to believe that Jesus is Messiah. But then the question suggests itself: if Roman Christians believe that Jesus is Messiah and Son of God, why write a gospel about what they already believe? There can be only one reason: to deepen their understanding of what they believe so that they can remain faithful to that belief.

Scholars have had little trouble in accepting the tradition that Mark writes to Christians in a condition of tension that challenges their faith. Mark writes to help a perplexed audience confronted by persecution for their beliefs. It is this perilous confrontation that motivates him to present Jesus, their Lord and savior, precisely as Messiah and Son of God. He thinks that if his readers will understand more perfectly what they profess when they say that Jesus is Messiah and Son of God, they will be better able to remain true to their faith till death.

An Introduction to Christ as Messiah

What are we to understand by "Messiah"? First, the fundamental or linguistic meaning of "Messiah" is "anointed", and implied in the term "anoint" is the material of anointing, oil. "Messiah" is an adjective with passive meaning; that is, someone or something has been anointed with oil by someone. In the Old Testament many and various people are said to have been were "anointed with the Holy Spirit": military leaders, kings, prophets, priests—all are described has having been "anointed with oil".

Though often a human being did the anointing of a king or a warrior, in most instances throughout the centuries of Israel's history it is God who anoints. Thus, "Messiah" becomes something of a code word; the person we call Messiah is one we recognize as anointed by God (At times the Spirit is indicated as the one who anoints.) As the term itself hints, and as one learns from the list of anointed people mentioned above, a person is anointed by God for a task. That task might be ruling, prophesying, fighting for Israel, leading the liturgy. In itself then it is rather generic in regard to its purpose. But in the gospels it has a specific meaning.

As far as the term itself is concerned, the word "Messiah" in relation to Jesus translates into Greek as "Christos", i.e., "Christ". This Greek form of the title took hold as Jesus' followers entered into the wider Mediterranean world (particularly in Antioch in Syria) where Greek was the normal and universal language. It is curious that the followers of Jesus were called, above all else, "Christians", i.e., "People of the Messiah". They must have preached in some form the idea that Jesus came as a result of God's love, a love destined to bring the goodness of God to each and every person of God's kingdom "through an anointed one". Jewish Christians would have to teach pagans what the term meant in Jewish history, but, once that was done, all believers could use the term "Messiah", or "Christ", of Jesus.

The Figure of the Royal Messiah in the Old Testament
Jewish writings, particularly the Old Testament, looked forward longingly for a time in which God would re-establish His authority over all powers, including that of Satan, and with it exercise His power to create His kingdom for His people. Many Jewish thinkers thought this kingdom would come about by a direct intervention of God alone. But many others thought that God would establish this kingdom through the agency of a human being, a king. Since this human being was thought of as king, according to tradition he would be "anointed". For Israel it is at the moment of anointing that one becomes a king: to call one "king" is to call him "the anointed one", and vice-versa. Thus, when Jesus in the gospels is called "Messiah of Israel" the implication is that he is "king of Israel". Given the political circumstances of the centuries before Jesus, this title meant that he was to re-establish Israel. The term points to a person who, as king,

would provide through his power, wisdom and fidelity to the Law of God all the good things associated with the kingdom. The goods are at hand. What is needed is a king, anointed in this case by God. In Jewish theology, it falls to God to choose the king, i.e., to anoint the Messiah. We are back at a time when monarchy, not democracy (nor the twelve tribes in political union), was the prevailing form of government in Israel. Thus an Israelite would have thought immediately of a king, if he wanted assurance that all people would receive this world's benefits. All hopes rested with the king.

In this political and social context, at first only a few, then many, began to think of Jesus as the Messiah, that is the one anointed by God to fulfill the hopes of everyone, to provide all good things of the kingdom. His miracles were especially powerful in arguing that Jesus is the one used by God to provide the fullness of the kingdom's blessings to all Israel. It is true that by Jesus' time, when Rome ruled the Mediterranean, there was no actual Jewish king, but the long-established hope of faith-filled Israelites was expressed by this archaic, but vibrant and precious title. Jews knew their tradition of anointing people for specific tasks. Often for momentous tasks. In the faith of Jewish Christians Jesus is regularly though of as being anointed by God to begin the kingdom and to rule over God's People. Given the expectations associated with the Messiah of bestowing blessings, one can easily understand why his beneficiaries refer to his coming as "good news".

Israel and Its Future

To understand more fully the title given Jesus, "the Messiah of Israel", it is valuable to review briefly Israel's centuries of life as a kingdom. Israel had nearly forty kings in its history between 1050 BC and 587 BC. All were anointed (or claimed to be anointed) to rule and provide benefits to their people. The idea of having a king or Messiah originally arose, not with God, but with the people. God had always been thought of as king of Israel—that there was no need of human kings. Israel insisted, however, that it wanted to be "like the other nations" (I Samuel 10, 17-19), and God relented, but only after a dire prediction of the failure of the monarchy. In a subsequent review of its history, Israel had to admit before God that it knew only two kings to be "good", Josiah and Hezekiah. All the rest were "evil" in whole or in part. Abusive and misused kingship, specifically, idol worship permitted by kings, was thought of as an insult to God that was responsible for the suffering of the people. If the king is evil, the good of the people and the worship of God will be ignored. So it was with Israel, the Old Testament says: because most of its kings chose evil and as a consequence the people chose evil as well, the kingdoms of the north (Israel [721 BC] and the south (Judah [587 BC]) were destroyed. This destruction was viewed as punishment from God for evil toward himself and for the subsequent injustices of people toward people as the law of God was ignored or ridiculed.

The Hope
But for all the pain and grief of the exiles, certain elements of Israel knew that its suffering was only punishment, not abandonment by God. They considered God's words in Psalm 89: "I will punish their offenses and scourge them on account of their guilt, but I will never take back my love.... I will never violate my covenant nor go back on the word I have spoken". These people knew in their hearts that God would one day put an end to his wrath and re-establish with Israel the covenant of good will. God would some day unilaterally re-enter Israel's life and offer again a union or perfect marriage that had been the hallmark of God's intentions towards his people. These Israelites, living in ashes, now lived too in hope. They waited and longed for and prayed for God's return to establish his kingdom, for, as they now knew, who could rule for their benefit more justly and lovingly than God? Yes, God had been angry and punitive because of the evil of Israel's shepherds. But now he would be their shepherd. And so, Israel looked for a new kingdom. Since many knew that God was ultimately king of Israel, they expected a king who would be human but who would be a true representative of God's love for his people. Meditating on their ancient and traditional experiences, they looked for the day when a king would again be appointed over them who was holy, wise and powerful. He would provide a kingdom in which Israel would enjoy the greatest blessings and perfection. When will he come? Because he most assuredly will!

Jesus As Messiah

And so it is no surprise to find many Israelites of the first century AD looking for a person of power, wisdom and holiness—for one about whom one can ask oneself, "Is he not the king? Has not God anointed him, after the manner of our long line of kings, to rule over us and bless us with prosperity? We long for the Messiah, is this not the one?"

The answer to this question for a number of Jews was that Jesus of Nazareth was this anointed one, Jesus was the long-awaited Messiah. One can expect from him a power and a wisdom and a holiness which define the Messiah, and many found these three characteristics in him. His miracles, his teaching and his fidelity to all aspects of Judaism are signs of his Messiahship. Indeed, looking to the gospels for a moment, we can say that if we wanted to argue the point that Jesus is Messiah, we would tell the story of Jesus in such a way as to highlight precisely these three characteristics of Messiah appeared in his life: wisdom, power, holiness. In short, for his followers Jesus is the longed-for hope for happiness and as such was identified by the term Messiah. For converts to a Christianity which was only in its beginning stages, the man with these three qualities is very appealing and deserves a following.

Jesus' View of the "Messiah"

Now for the peculiar slant of Mark in regard to Jesus the Messiah. There is little doubt that Mark presents, in his first eight chapters, a Jesus who has the hallmarks of the Messiah: power, wisdom and holiness. While Mark does not record much of Jesus' teaching, in addition to his parables, what we do find in Chapters 10 and 11 are adequate signs of his wisdom. Mark's gospel abounds in miracles, indicators of the total perfection and benefit Jesus could bring to mankind. Finally, Jesus is described at prayer, and his intense desire for and union with his Father is amply shown in his fidelity to his Father in his temptations in the desert, in his integrity and love of God and neighbor, in his dedication to his life's work, and in his devotion to his Father's will in his agony in the garden. In this presentation Mark makes sure his reader recognizes Jesus as rich in those qualities which indicate him to be the king who will bless Israel perfectly. Mark also makes sure that his reader, already a believer, already a Christian, renews his appreciation of Jesus, a wise, powerful and holy messiah. Indeed, one might even assume that, though the Christians of Rome professed Jesus to be a king, the Messiah, they did not know all the stories and sayings that Mark reports to them, stories and sayings by which their faith in Jesus, now more fully informed, would significantly increase. Most of all, from this first half of Mark they would understand Jesus as Mark thinks best for the solution to their problems.

The Death of Jesus as Contradiction

But, there is more to the story of Jesus than miracles and wisdom and holiness. Jesus died a terrible death, a death over which he appears to have no power (he did not save himself), no wisdom (he did not outthink his accusers) and no holiness (he would be known by many as guilty of a capital crime). The problem now shifts. Since one cannot deny the power, wisdom and holiness of his public life (Mark makes very sure that no one can), no longer is there a question as to whether or not Jesus qualifies to be called the longed-for anointed one or Messiah. It is now a question of how can one who has the power and wisdom and holiness of the messiah meet such a contradictory end. Is this crucified man Messiah? Can we still call him that? Not according to any of the traditional qualities that define the Messiah, the anointed king; no tradition within Judaism ever expected the eternally beneficent kingdom to be ruled by a Messiah who died powerless, as a fool, as a criminal. In thinking about God's kingdom and its unending benefits, such an expectation is contradictory and ludicrous: indeed, does not his inglorious death put an end to such a title?

Yet, crucifixion, Mark claimed, is just as much a part of this Jesus as are the qualities of wisdom, power and holiness. One must learn to re-define "Messiah". Once the Christian in Rome can do that, once he can integrate the Messianic qualities of Jesus with his horrible end, he is ready to confront his own crises. He can now re-define not only Jesus, but himself as a follower of a powerful, wise and holy Messiah who dies without defending power, without winning argument, without approval of the law. Like him, the follower must be ready to die ignominiously, unjustly, if he is to follow the Messiah; "he must be ready to take up his cross and follow me". With this deeper understanding of his powerful Messiah and with this readiness to die if that is asked of him, the Roman Christian can confront the challenges to his faith while still convinced that Jesus will lead him to the eternal good called "the kingdom of God". Mark writes to spell out the meaning of Messiah (and of Son of God), but always with the goal to help his reader live his Christian dedication to Christ as thoroughly as possible.

Peter

Consider this example. Jesus asked his disciples, "Who do you say I am?" Peter answered for himself (and no doubt for the other eleven), "You are the Messiah". Then in just a few moments Jesus began to predict his imminent betrayal and death, indeed crucifixion, to which Peter responds more or less in these words, "That is impossible!" Why, in the eyes of Peter, is such a death impossible for the Messiah? Why has Peter failed to understand how crucifixion and humiliation, suffered for one's beliefs, cannot be part of being a messiah and of following the Messiah? He can think this way because he has a seriously deficient, if not entirely incorrect, understanding of who God's Messiah truly is.

If that is true of Peter, it is also true of the community for whom Mark writes his gospel. That community did not enjoy a way of thinking about Jesus that later communities such as ours of the twenty-first century have grown accustomed to. Granted that Mark's readers have dedicated themselves to Jesus, they do not have a tradition to fall back on for support and explanation, nor the depth of understanding of the person to whom they are committed which will allow them to suffer for his name. This early first-century community must realize fully what it professes when it says that Jesus of Nazareth is the Messiah. The community needs to hear once again, now within a context of its own suffering for the name of Jesus, that its messiah laid down his life for the truth and in fidelity to his Father, and so then should they.

Thus, it is no accident that, immediately after Jesus predicts his own crucifixion, Mark has Jesus teach that anyone following him must be ready to take up his cross, too. Herein lies Mark's particular teaching about the Messiah: he must die, even though powerful, wise and holy; and the disciple must also be ready to accept, while admitting Jesus is wise and holy and powerful, that the disciple, too, can at the same time suffer and die for his commitment to Jesus. This is the meaning which we must understand at the first line of the gospel of Mark. This is the good news of Jesus, powerful, wise and holy, but nonetheless crucified. Put in another way, Mark, with a view to the persecutions Christians were undergoing, told the story of Jesus' adult life in such a way as to underline the apparently contradictory qualities of Jesus, the glorious one of God, but the humiliated and crucified one, too. Can a disciple learn that faith in Jesus messiah might include suffering as well as glory and happiness? Can the disciple realize that he is called to manifest in joy or suffering, like Jesus, total devotion to one's calling, which is the worship of God in the Christian's religious words and actions?

A Further Consideration about Mark's Audience

Another thought (which we have already introduced) to be woven into what we have already said is this: Mark is writing to people who already believe that Jesus is Messiah. At least twenty years before Mark wrote, Paul had readily, easily called Jesus "Messiah" or "Christ". This title is used throughout Paul's letters and indeed it is so common a term for Jesus that "Christ" has become his name. Moreover, we should not say that Paul was the first one to call Jesus Messiah; he no doubt learned of Jesus as Messiah from earlier Christians influenced by the beginning preachers from Jerusalem. Mark was not introducing his audience to a new term they had not heard before—Mark's first verse is not a view which the audience does not already embrace. They are Christians before Mark writes and have been instructed in what to believe: Mark presents the title of Messiah in his first verse with no explanation, presuming that every one of his readers was well acquainted with "Messiah". Indeed no writing of the New Testament is addressed to non-Christians, and every New Testament author presumes his audience is Christian (as every community believes the author is Christian). No New Testament document was ever written to convert people to Christianity.

Thus, since we put Mark's Gospel at about 70 AD, we can only affirm that, probably having heard about Pauline teaching since 50 AD, many of his readers already believed that Jesus was the Messiah; indeed, as we have said, it is most reasonable to say that "Christians" had expressed a belief in Jesus as Messiah for years before Paul wrote. With this in mind, then, we have every reason to think that Mark wanted to make sure that these Christians understood more profoundly and exactly just who this person was to whom they had dedicated their lives. Ancient titles like Messiah summed up valuable experiences in Jesus' life, as he frequently showed the Messiah's power and wisdom and holiness according to traditional expectation, but the complete understanding of the Messiah was an understanding that he was Messiah to the end, in accord with the intentions of the One Who had anointed him. Moreover, the understanding of Jesus is the means to make sense of their own lives, which, like that of Jesus, were threatened with oppression and even death, all because of their faith in Jesus. If they understand Jesus properly, they will understand that suffering for him does not remove his power to make them happy, for suffering has been intertwined with glory to make up the new definition of messiah and of those committed to him.

It is all of Jesus' adult life, glorious but full of opposition and finally so unexpectedly and brutally terminated, and it is this life, together with its "pleasant parts", which calls for explanation and integration. Certainly parts of that life give every reason to think of him in the traditional sense of Messiah. But another and all-absorbing part of his life calls for a redefinition that will include among the characteristics of Messiah a tragic and apparently senseless death. Christians had to hear who their Messiah truly is, what obedience to God truly is, then see themselves as his followers, certainly for glory, and, given the world's opposition to God, probably for suffering.

Suffering, But Then Glory

We understand better now how we are to appraise the revelations by which Jesus identified himself. Perceiving now the full understanding of the meaning of Messiah, one has instant comprehension that the Messiah, traditionally expected to bring the kingdom, has been anointed to rule, but only at a later time, after his death. Mark will explain that Jesus understands himself not as a ruler, at least not now, but as an anointed to call people to the kingdom by repentance. One can say that the kingdom has begun with Jesus—we need only look at the wonders and wisdom by which he has improved the world. But we long for all the blessings to be given us and know very well that they are to come only after our deaths. In the meantime, and in accord with the Old Testament understanding of God, one must repent in order to enter that wonderful kingdom to which Jesus by teaching, and then by obedience has preceded us. However, this call to repentance, which involves teaching people how the repentant person should live, will bring trouble and death to Jesus. There are many of his generation who think Jesus a traitor to the traditions of Judaism, particularly in what they consider his rather frivolous disobedience towards traditions regarding the sabbath and his disregard for the many traditional laws of purity or cleanliness. Thus, for Mark, the anointing of Jesus means that we have a king who is anointed to preach the kingdom and urge entry into it. But Jesus was unable to deny or remain silent about what he knows to be the nature of this kingdom: he is the Messiah anointed to be crucified. Like the Christian, Jesus was anointed at baptism. Like the Christian, he was given the task of witnessing to God, which, in Jesus' case was spelled out essentially by preaching repentance, by teaching, and by accepting the consequences of his teaching, even to death on a cross. Was not life in its ultimate reality a carrying out of the will of God, however that divine was to be spelled out for him and for his followers?

Defining Jesus as Messiah

The notion of Messiah begins Mark's gospel, and then faithfully follows Jesus until its ending. How do we spell that out? In the first eight chapters of the gospel, Mark slowly, inexorably, even enthusiastically builds up an experience of Jesus which ends with Peter's correct insight: "You are the Messiah" (Mark 8, 29): "you have filled every criterion we have for identifying the promised Messiah". It is only after this Petrine declaration, i.e., after Mark has solidly confirmed that Jesus is wise, powerful and holy as was no one else in Israel, that Mark chooses to introduce the words of Jesus that announce his death and resurrection. Given the positioning of this announcement about the end of his life, it seems right to say that now, after Jesus' many miracles, we must think principally about his mysterious death which seems not to fit with the first half of the gospel. To introduce the subject of rejection and death and resurrection, Jesus employs about himself not the term "Messiah", but the title "son of man". This choice of Jesus points to the figure in Daniel, Chapter 7, where we find the "one like a son of man" who is given the responsibility which rightfully belongs to God of judging human beings. This judgment belongs to God for it a occurs at the end of the ages and is the entry point to eternal life. In this chapter of Daniel it becomes clear that the figure who will make these judgments as the king of a heavenly kingdom will judge only after he has suffered. The "son of man" was a figure known for his humiliation and subsequent glorification. Thus, it is this figure upon which Jesus calls to help his disciples understand the otherwise incomprehensible end of the Messiah: Jesus, after being humiliated and crucified, will end in glory.

But this Danielic figure of a son of man, so expressive of the movement from suffering to glory, did not explain completely the sense of Jesus' death. For this, Mark made clear use (without expressing the title) of the suffering servant in Isaiah, particularly in Chapters 52–53. This sinless servant, in obedience to God, goes to death silently and without resistance so that others, sinners, may go free and unpunished. It is the second half of the gospel which emphasizes this figure. Weaving the son of man image with that of the servant, Jesus notes after his third prediction of Jesus' passion (all these predictions are in the second half of the gospel): "...the son of man...has come to give his life as a ransom for many" (10, 45). At times, so great is the concentration of the gospel on Jesus' death, one wonders if Jesus' coming was *uniquely* to give his life as a ransom for many.

But even the figure of the son of man/servant gives way finally to another image, indeed the image which both closes Mark's description of Jesus in the words of the centurion at the cross (15, 39) and begins it (1, 1): "Son of God". "Son of God'" is used now to explain how it is that the Messiah will quietly, determinedly accept humiliation, betrayal, punishments, injustice and crucifixion, and will necessarily rise from all this to life again. The Messiah, powerful, wise and holy, will now show through his filial obedience, the obedience of the Son to his Father, how it is that the messiah embraced death.

Son of God
As often happens, the more mysterious something is, the more intense its presentation. While the title "Son of God" is given to many kinds of people (and angels) in the Jewish tradition, it means only "divine" in the gospel of Mark. I say "divine" in the sense of signifying the divinity of Jesus. The first century Christians early believed that Jesus was divine: what we have in the scriptures are attempts to make that faith in his divinity ever more intelligible. (Consider the words of St. John of the Cross: "...Holy doctors have uncovered many mysteries and wonders...Jesus is like a mine with many pockets containing treasures; however deep we dig, we will never find their end or their limit".) To the best of their abilities, early Christians tried, in any number of ways, to explain what they knew to be true: Jesus is divine. We see such a way when we turn to writings well

before Mark's gospel—the Pauline letters. These letters, particularly Romans, Ephesians, Colossians and Philippians, show the kinds of effort people earlier than Mark put into trying to explain what is unique and ultimately, as the centuries have shown, fully inexplicable to the human mind. Consider the words of the Letter to the Philippians: "...he was in the form of God.... he emptied himself, coming in human likeness" (2, 6-7), or the words of Colossians: "He is the image of the invisible God, the firstborn of all creation; in him were created all things...all things were created through him and for him" (1, 15-16). Still earlier, Paul had cited the faith of Christians: "...one God, the Father, from whom all things exist...and one Lord, Jesus Christ, through whom all things are and through whom we exist" (I Corinthians 8, 6). The statements that we find in Paul are not perfect, and later generations will try to make them better. But, though we still do not have the perfect understanding and expression of Jesus as divine, we know him to be that and profess it. And so the mystery remains.

Given the belief of Christian writers and Christian audiences in the divinity of Jesus that characterized the decades before Mark wrote, we can easily say that Mark presumes from the beginning of his gospel that his reader believes Jesus is aptly called Son of God in the fully divine sense. Thus, his gospel is not meant to prove that Jesus is Son of God; at best, the gospel will serve to give particular insight into the meaning of Jesus Son of God, since it serves to reveal the fullness involved in the initial profession: Jesus is Messiah. Since, however, Mark forces the reader at the very beginning of the gospel to think of Jesus as divine by putting there this identification (and not, for instance, "son of man" or "Lord" or "savior"), we ask why Mark did this, or what exactly is his particular slant in using this title.

The puzzling event in the public life of Jesus is his death. His was no calm passing from this life, his was a brutal ending. A key to understanding the tragedy of that night and the subsequent day is the story of the agony in the garden. In this garden, as Mark describes the event, two factors stand out. First, we note the pleas of Jesus that his disciples stay awake and pray not to enter into testing. Indeed, Mark's gospel is concerned to have the disciple ready and prompt to "take up his cross and follow me". Since his audience is being oppressed because of its belief in Jesus, Mark knows the audience needs to hear these words of command.

Second, we read the central and most suggestive prayer: "Father, if it be possible, let this cup of suffering pass from me; yet not my will, but yours be done". There is a relationship expressed and underlined here, a relationship of Father to Son; Jesus recognizes himself as Son of this Father. And it is this relationship that is the basis of Jesus' request and final acquiescence. He appeals to God as Father; he knows what his Father wants; he does not want to do it, but will do it, if the Father wishes.

Once Jesus rises from his prayerful position, he is absolutely confident that whatever will happen now will be his Father's will to which Jesus, as Son, is to be obedient. Therein lies the special meaning of "Son of God" that begins Mark's gospel. Mark, presuming that his reader confess Jesus to be essentially divine, wants to emphasize to his reader how Jesus, as truly Son, obeys his Father, even in a matter Jesus abhors. This filial obedience, expressed in the garden, characterizes the person of Jesus, and, in these circumstances, explains his silence throughout the rest of the passion narrative. It is to this aspect of Jesus' divine sonship that Mark calls the attention of his reader from the very beginning of a story he knows must end with tragic, painful death. To finish his presentation, Mark describes a pagan Roman centurion who, while not knowing anything of Jesus' divinity, does recognize that Jesus' death was that of a loyal and faithful son to his Father; his pagan testimony witnesses to Jesus' total and filial obedience. Jesus, the centurion's testimony says, did not deserve to die, but died because his Father asked him to. He died out of religious obedience.

Will the reader learn from that obedience to be likewise a child of God in obedience, even if the Father asks him to accept suffering? In other words, the Christian by baptism is a child of God. What then should be the attitude of the Christian to the Father's will? Jesus becomes the model of a Christian's life, even to accepting humiliation and death for fidelity to God and His teaching, if the Father calls for it. Like Jesus, the Christian is called upon to be nothing less than an obedient child of God.

We say that the latter part of Jesus' life—his passion, death and resurrection—is best understood as the will of a Father accepted wholeheartedly by a Son. This means that the mention of Son of God in verse 1 looks to its employment in the last chapters of the gospel. But if "Son of God" is designed to introduce Jesus as obedient to his Father in the grimmest of circumstances, can we not say retrospectively that Jesus, thoroughly obedient for all of his public life, expressed his divine Sonship at the beginning of the Marcan story and not only at its end? Son of God is a title used to explain the end of the story, but it really is validly applied to interpret the entire life of Jesus, which is ultimately a life of obedience. It is in the light of this total obedience of Jesus throughout his public life that one best understands the event which stands at the beginning of Jesus' public life: his baptism (1, 9-11). In this experience, God identifies Jesus as My Son, My beloved. With the grammatical emphasis given the word "beloved" and the repetition involved in the words "in whom I am well pleased" we have further reference to the servant, now as he is described in Isaiah 42, 1. The servant will carry out the will of God in preaching repentance to Israel (and indeed to the entire world). This allusion to Isaiah will be repeated again, before the passion, in the transfiguration of Jesus. In short, it is as the obedient servant that the Son, known to be divine, will demonstrate an essential quality of Son: obedience to his Father.

Jesus' Divinity in Mark

I have stressed obedience as the basic significance of the title Son of God for Mark's readers; they, too, must realize that being a baptized child of God means obedience, even in the direst of circumstances. This stress on obedience is necessary to answer the problems of Mark's community, but there is undoubtedly more to say about Jesus as divine in the gospel.

We have emphasized the fact that the Messiahship of Jesus, even though qualified by his humiliation and powerlessness in death, is clearly discernible in the first eight chapters of the gospel. In these chapters Jesus shows himself to be powerful, holy and wise—characteristics of the Messiah. But when one sounds these chapters to seek their fullest revelation, one cannot help but wonder, as did the apostles, "Who but God can work these miracles?" Who could order about the demonic powers, calm the waves and the wind, feed five thousand people with five loaves of bread, make whole the blind and the lame, and even forgive sins? Indeed, these acts show power and thus indicate the Messiah, but in their deepest meaning they also show the presence of the divine. Mark's readers, who already believe Jesus is divine, need no proof of that fact here, but they do recognize divinity in their Messiah, their Christ, and they should never, despite how his life ends, forget this divine aspect of their Lord. Indeed, it can further be said that though one initially believes Jesus is divine, the recounting of his power and wisdom can only strengthen this faith. And so, the lesson to be learned from this gospel is not that Jesus is simply divine, but that he is the obedient divine Son of his Father.

Conclusion

Mark's gospel certainly intends to deepen the believer's conviction that Jesus is Messiah of Israel: Mark's recounting of stories which manifest the holiness, power and wisdom of the Messiah drives home the assurance that Jesus is Messiah in the tradition of Son of David. But one notices that already at Chapter 3, 6 there is nefarious and unjustified plotting to kill Jesus. As Jesus manifests his identity so as to merit the traditional title of Messiah, Mark calls attention to the opposition to Jesus which will eventually demand a rethinking of the meaning of Messiah. If Jesus is Messiah, Messiah must be someone who is crucified, and that was hard for the disciples of Jesus to understand, especially if the disciple's life follows the pattern of Jesus' life.

To identify Jesus as Messiah this way means to identify what it means to be a follower of Jesus: one who will enjoy the benefits of a powerful, holy and wise leader, but also one who will need the virtue of faith to remain loyal to Jesus. By Chapter 8, 34 Mark has made clear this nuanced meaning of Jesus which his audience must respect: "the son of man must be handed over...".

Once he passes this midpoint of the gospel, Mark turns his attention more fully to the inevitable crucifixion and its implication for the disciple. Few are the miracles now, and little is the teaching (except that which reflects a "carrying of the cross"), and there is little record of great crowds following Jesus. Now, with open talk of crucifixion, it is time to introduce the reader to the fate of Jesus, first under the Danielic title of son of man, then, more importantly, under the title of Son of God, a title which will reveal how obedient, from baptism to death, Jesus the Son was to his Father. Neither "Son of God" nor "Messiah" implied humiliation followed by glorification; that sequence comes from his title as son of man. But once Mark has shown that the Messiah prophesizes three times about his destiny, it is time to show how that Messiah accepts his fearsome fate with the obedience of the Son toward his Father. Thus this is a story about a Messiah who is the divine Son of God and the obedient Son of God. There is a somber atmosphere of anticipation now, especially as the follower learns that he, too, must be ready to carry the cross. There is not much moral teaching in Mark, but there is emphasis on the disciple's charity and on his humility and fidelity in imitation of Jesus who is humble and faithful. The imminent persecution which ends the life of the Messiah helps set the tone for talk of future persecutions of disciples and the defense against them. Never a part of the glorious first "Messianic" half of the gospel, persecution is a reality of future discipleship that should be addressed in this half of the gospel.

Mark thinks he can tell the story of Jesus in such a way as to solidify faith in the powerful, wise and holy Jesus, and in the same story, show how his being Messiah has to include crucifixion for his beliefs, i.e., how being Son, Jesus the Messiah will be obedient to the Father, even if it means a horrible death. The story of Jesus, then, should strengthen faith in the glorious king who will bring all perfection to his believers, while the story reveals the deepest meanings of the one in whom the Christian believes. The story was to be told in such a way that Christians could be positive that they are following the holy, powerful and wise Messiah, and yet absorb into their understanding of Jesus the reasons why he suffered and why he remained so silent and unchallenging, right to his death. Christians should know how obediently he acted in suffering for his own beliefs, and hear his words that can inspire the readers to an obedience which underlined every one of Jesus' acts.

Mark signals right from the start that he wants to tell a story about a Messiah who is wonderful, yet suffers as a Son can be expected to suffer who is willing to die to do his Father's will. Mark's few words of introduction set the tone for a gospel of encouragement in ever stronger faith in Jesus, whether from his words or deeds, or from his death and resurrection. Jesus was one destined to suffer for his belief and asked to obey so as to give witness to the truth. In that, he is not very different from Mark's reader, who suffered for the truth, suffered for his belief. It is to be a solace and encouragement to the suffering Christian that the Messianic Jesus in Mark suffers so tragically even to say, as the Christian might, "Why have you forsaken me?" (15, 34). Jesus, the Messiah who lived always as Son, remains trusting in his Father, and can only ask "why?" If such a question is in the mind of the reader, so too is the confidence that Jesus had in his Father, a confidence that overcomes all hesitation and inspires full faith. In times of persecution, it is most helpful to think of Jesus as Messiah and Son of God.

* * * * *

It is particularly beneficial to note the structure Mark uses to make clear the meaning of Jesus, Messiah and Son of God: the adult life of Jesus occurs only in the north of Palestine, and only at the end of it does Jesus go south to Jerusalem. As far as we know, the structure or outline is Mark's and is a sign of the freedom with which the author deals with his material. Whereas he no doubt inherited from many sources the stories he tells, it is he who put them into the outline that structures his gospel. Moreover, Mark's structure is noteworthy because it serves for both of the basic structures of Matthew and Luke. Such was Mark's influence on the two later gospels.

Mark's Introduction in Context

Mark's gospel offers a story along these lines: there is a presentation of John the Baptist, followed by personal experiences of Jesus (i.e., baptism and temptation), which in turn open onto a public life of Jesus that is, at first, centered in Galilee (consider 10, 1, which announces Jesus' intention to leave Galilee for Jerusalem), then in the area around Jerusalem. In a sense we can say that Mark kept Jesus in Galilee till it was time for him to face his destiny in Jerusalem. Perhaps this Marcan decision is artificial; certainly John the Evangelist does not have Jesus visit Jerusalem only once—he goes a number of times to visit the city. But whoever has the data right, Mark has the advantage of drama: Jesus will visit the holy city only one time and that is to die. The reader, of course, is quite aware of Jesus' death in Jerusalem, and so can be presumed to know the end and to be waiting for it to occur. Mark wants him to wait for a while; first he must tell some stories.

Mark's Presentation of John the Baptist

The first Marcan decision we come upon is a presentation, not of Jesus, but of John the Baptist. Basically, John is offered as one who calls his generation to repentance and foretells the coming of one "greater than I", the one whom Mark has already introduced as Messiah and Son of God. John disappears from the scene quickly, but his witness carries forward: one is coming who is "greater than I". Presumably this new person will, like John, ask Israel for repentance. This person who is about to arrive is not identified here with the terms which Mark offers in his introduction (Messiah, Son of God). Yet, the "one greater than I", the "one who is to come"—that figure will soon change into the classic titles used by Mark for Jesus: Messiah (Christ) and Son of God (with help from the title, son of man, when Mark speaks about the passion of Jesus). The peculiarity of beginning the gospel story with John and not Jesus is explained by the fact that as far as the evangelists and early Christians understood things, the divine plan of God to save everyone began, not with Jesus, but with the one who foretold the coming of Jesus and gave him identity. Mark's insight into the divine will is what justifies his beginning a gospel with John. In John we first find God. For centuries Israel felt it no longer heard the word of God through His prophets. Now, through John, God again addresses Israel, and through John, God declares: Israel should ready herself to prepare for "one greater than I". (A secondary reason for beginning with John is to make clear the superiority of Jesus and the relative inferiority of John.)

Jesus' Preparation for His Public Life

With John's witness in place, Mark chooses two stories to prepare us for the public life of Jesus. The first story is an account of Jesus' experience at his baptism. Jesus, like all pious Jews, wants to express public sorrow for sins so as to have a life filled with God. At the moment of Jesus' completing his baptism, the Spirit of God descends on him and the voice from on high identifies himself to Jesus. We note that from this moment forward, the Spirit inspires Jesus in all he says and does. Indeed, the Spirit is poured out in this very special moment in the history of humanity only on Jesus, and, as the Gospel says, it is this Spirit which now guides Jesus. After his resurrection from the dead, Jesus will give the Spirit to all believers.

The second part of the baptism story tells of God's words addressed to Jesus. In them Jesus is called "My Son, My beloved Son". As mentioned earlier, there is no doubt that writer and reader alike know Jesus to be divine, the Son of God. Here the emphasis is rather on the fact that the Father is giving full recognition to Jesus' willingness to obey Him, as a son obeys his father. The implication is far-reaching: all that follows, all that Jesus does and says, is the fulfillment of what he knows to be his Father's will. Indeed, his very Messiahship is an act of obedience to the Father. We have been prepared for this divine obedience by the introduction.

Then Mark gives us a second account: Jesus' experience of forty days in the desert, a preparation for his ministry and tragic end. In this experience, though he is tempted by Satan, animals and angels protects him and we can presume that he gathers the strength to do what his Father wants him to do. Mark probably told this story in such a way as to remind us of Psalm 91 which assures God's protection for his loved one, and of the figure of Adam who lived in peace with all animals before he sinned. Jesus, then, is the new Adam.

One should emphasize that Mark does not consider Jesus a sinner in need of repentance and baptism, but as one who shows his visible support for the preaching of John to repent and be baptized. Again, obedience and sorrow for sin are the continued theme.

Jesus As Son of David

The second Marcan division runs from 1, 14 to the departure for Jerusalem in 10, 1. Within this section, a bit more than one half of the gospel, Mark chooses to report a variety of stories about Jesus. The underlying thread which unites them all (for, as far as we know, most all of them were not linked together before this) is the presentation of Jesus in such a way that we are led to the fundamental question in 8, 27-29, "Who do people say I am?" and Peter's perceptive response, "You are the Christ". In other words, the plan of Mark is so to present Jesus that the reader (always a believer) can agree with Peter's assessment of the Jesus of the first 8 chapters. To this end, we have many miracles reported, in which one sees the complete domination of Jesus over the demon world, nature, death, mental sickness, physical deformity, even forgiveness of sin. We hear the wisdom of Jesus as he responds to the teachers of Israel and see his closeness to his Father in his seeking him "in deserted places".

Mark 2–9 and the Introduction

In Mark 2–9 we are led to realize as early as 3, 6 that prominent religious people want Jesus dead. For them, his teaching is false and thus dangerous for Israel. It is for the reader to intervene and say that, on the contrary, what the reader has heard is wisdom, not foolishness. For all that, the destiny of Jesus is already set: he must die.

Jesus' power and his personal life of prayer argue for his holiness: such power as he revealed could not be any other than the power associated with God Himself. This first section reinforces the belief of the reader that indeed Jesus is Messiah, for he has the characteristics expected of the Messiah by Jewish tradition: supreme power, wisdom and holiness.

Early in these opening chapters we see both the gathering of disciples and the theme of Jesus' preaching and teaching for the gospel's remaining eight chapters. His disciples are not just students of the teacher, for they do not simply learn, but they leave all and follow him. They wander with him, live with him. However important and striking are the miracles of Jesus as they show him to be Messiah and Son of God, more important and lasting is his constant call to repentance from sin and belief in himself. The end of time is indeed near. One can call to repentance in just a few minutes, but it takes days to teach what full repentance means. Thus the teaching of Jesus, with its similes and metaphors and parables and one-line authoritative statements and proverbs, with its support by miracles of all sorts, is a teaching that is, in one way or another, to be subsumed under his lasting call to repentance. Why does he preach repentance and the teaching that belongs to it? Jesus makes clear that his life is dedicated to announcing the presence of the kingdom of God and to preparing people to enter it by repentance and true virtue. Such a calling is the will of God, and, upon reflection, bolsters the belief that Jesus is the Messiah, for this Messiah, through his teaching about repentance, assures the certain happiness of the kingdom. It is through this change of heart that one will enter into the world of the wonderful blessings expected for centuries from the Messiah. Thus, everything in these eight chapters shows Jesus as the hope for all who want the greatest blessings of the longed-for kingdom. True to his baptismal experience, Jesus shows himself "My Son, my beloved Son, willing to do My will; in him is all My delight", for by his obedience the will of God that all be saved, can come to fruition.

Thus, to call Jesus Messiah because of his power and wisdom and holiness (as Peter does) is insufficient. The Messiah must also die, in conditions which seem to deny the qualities of Messiah.

In Mark Jesus remains in Galilee till 10, 1. Between Peter's act of faith that Jesus is Messiah (8, 29) and Jesus' departure for Jerusalem, Mark presents the *conundrum extraordinaire*. Jesus uses the figure of the son of man, who by definition must first suffer, only then to be glorified. Using the figure of the son of man Jesus addresses the events at the end of his life. These events will throw into great doubt the assured conviction that Jesus is Messiah. Yes, he has shown he has the characteristics of Messiah, but how can such power, wisdom and holiness be reduced to the impotence, foolishness and criminality of a person crucified? What kind of Messiah is that? Why continue to hope in him?

In 8, 29 – 10, 1 we have stories which are of three types. First, there are stories in which Jesus (twice) predicts his terrible death, followed by resurrection; the reaction to these predictions varies from sadness to disappointment to total confusion, especially as reference to the resurrection seems to be ignored. Second, there are stories which serve to underline the fact that, if one intends to follow Jesus, one must be prepared to carry one's own cross. These stories include teachings which show what the cross can mean in a Christian's life of virtue. Indeed, it is within the presentation of the cross that Mark has Jesus speak of the key virtues of humility and charity. Is not the practice of these two virtues often a carrying of the cross? Finally, there are stories that continue, within this new aura of impending tragedy, a vision of Jesus' goodness. These stories must mean that Jesus died innocently, unjustly, and that one must look more deeply into his life for an explanation of his death. The death is other than it appears.

Mark has introduced Jesus as obedient Messiah (Christ) and, thereby obedient Son of God. Having looked at the first half of the gospel, we can see how Mark's introduction sums up Mark's effort to show through story form that Jesus is Messiah in the traditional sense. And Son of God, even if Messiah and Son of God must now include death by crucifixion.

Mark 10–16 and the Introduction

The second half of the gospel is dedicated to anticipating and then presenting the death of Jesus as a death of obedience. This is a radical change in the gospel narrative. Now there will be only two miracles. Both involve blindness and stand for symbols of the disciples' incomprehension about what is to come. There is further teaching, about love of neighbor and about humility, hard teaching. For what Jesus demands is often difficult, indeed even a cross. There are not large crowds rushing to hear Jesus. The story is severely limited to Jesus and the closest disciples. The atmosphere of joy and glory and wonder is for the most part gone. In its place there is anxiety and puzzlement. The story of the transfiguration reminds the reader not to forget during the grief that is to come the glory of Jesus. The image of the suffering son of man, which fills out the description of Jesus as Messiah, now becomes dominant.

Once the reader reaches Chapter 11 he faces the strange story of Jesus' entry into Jerusalem. It is a perplexing event, for while most of the onlookers think of Jesus' ride as a statement that he is now intends to overthrow Roman dominance and free Jerusalem, it is in reality a proclamation that he is truly Messianic as he understands the term. According to Jesus' understanding of Messiah he is powerful and holy and wise, Jesus spends a number of days teaching in Jerusalem after his triumphal entry. His locale is no longer Galilee but the holy city. Here Mark presents a cycle of stories, each of which evidences the wisdom of Jesus under attack from the obstinate opponents: Pharisees, Sadducees, scribes and the priestly family. He shows himself a capable adversary of these Jerusalem opponents. He even perplexes them when they cannot answer a question he puts to them. The sense that Jesus is the wise Messiah continues to grow.

Finally, Mark presents the last hours of Jesus. These include a kind of teaching previously not heard from Jesus: the warning to prepare for the final judgment, to repent, and to persevere to the end. These hours include an anointing in preparation for Jesus' death and the organization of his capture. We also have a dinner at which Jesus announces the shocking news that Peter, the one who had called Jesus Messiah, will deny even knowing him. Another is a lesson that interprets his imminent death: "This is my body...this is my blood by which the New Covenant with God will be established, my blood shed for all people". These words give the deepest meaning to the death of the Messiah, Son of God.

With the agony in the garden we find the key to Jesus' attitude as he faces trial and then death. He reveals himself as Son of the Father. Clearly this story shows that he does not want to die, but equally that he wants to obey. He is true Son, not simply in the sense of one who is divine, but in the sense of a Son obedient to his Father. Knowing this about him, one can understand Jesus' silence in the face of his accusers, in the face of those who ridicule him, in the face of his pain. As Jesus dies he asks His Father why He does not intercede on his behalf. The only answer Mark gives is the Father's divine act of raising His obedient Son to life, unending life.

It is that the centurion in charge of the crucifixion calls Jesus "Son of God". In one sense the centurion can be understood to represent the many pagans who will become converts to Christianity between the time of Jesus' death and the writing of Mark's gospel. In another sense he is meant to be an unbiased witness about the character of Jesus: in my judgment, he says that this crucified one acted as an obedient son of God. We cannot say that the centurion believed that Jesus was divine, but he does unwittingly use the title that best describes Jesus.

The story of the empty tomb reinforces both the uniqueness of Jesus and the continuing perplexity of his disciples. Jesus does not appear to his disciples in this final story of Mark's original Gospel (16, 1-8). Here Mark is telling a story that corresponds to the experience of many of his Christian readers: in 70 AD in Rome they have not seen the risen Lord either; they hear the announcement, but wait, still wait for the appearance. Before what one sees and hears, the proper attitude is that of Israel before its God: reverential fear and confession that we have without doubt experienced a mighty act of God.

We have developed a bit more completely what Mark had indicated was his essential interest in telling the story of Jesus to Christians suffering for their faith in Rome. They need to understand rightly what it means that Jesus is Messiah and Son of God and the implications for a disciple who wants to follow such a Messiah who must die and such a Son who must be obedient to the will of his Father.

Another writer added to Mark's Gospel a second and longer account of events connected to the resurrection of Jesus. This account tells of appearances of Jesus to various disciples: we now know that he is alive! And this account talks about the future after Jesus' return to his Father: in one sense gone, Jesus will continue to work to make preaching firm and to do this with signs that can only move people to complete faith and trust in him.

If one were to read the gospel of Mark without its first verse, one might come to the conclusions Mark hopes will follow from his story. But the reader's effort to understand will more surely reach the goal Mark intends for him if he knows before the action begins that Mark wants to direct his thought to a deeper appreciation of the Jesus in whom he believes: Jesus as Messiah and Son of God.

John

John's gospel has an introduction (often called the prologue) of eighteen verses (John 1, 1-8). John says, at the original end of his gospel, that what he has written has been written "so that you may continue to believe that Jesus is Messiah, the Son of God, and that believing you may have unending life" (20, 30-31). Given the aim of his gospel, that one believe so as to have life, it is fitting that the introduction present God to the reader precisely as the source of life, indeed of all that exists. With God, the Word-made-flesh is involved in the existence of the world, in that he is identified as the one through whom the God of Israel created everything that is. Thus, since the Word eventually becomes flesh and is named Jesus, through Jesus comes life. The public life of Jesus, told in powerful stories and speeches, is, for John, to be seen as an aid to deepen the Christian's belief and hope that he will possess life: one who believes in Jesus will not lie dead forever. This life is not simply immortality, but fulfillment and love and everlasting joy with the love of one's whole being.

Actually, the eighteen verses, most of which basically can be said to make up a poem, are in part an introduction to the figure of John the Baptist and in part comments from the author inserted into the poem. Specifically, John the Baptist is mentioned in verses 6-9 and 15; the non-poetic comments of the author are in verses 12b-13 and 17-18. What is said of John the Baptist can be explained by what we say later in the gospel of Luke. Now we concentrate on Jesus, and how the evangelist chose to present him. But to better understand John's way of introducing Jesus as the cause of all that exists and as the source of life, we must recall the intellectual atmosphere of John's time (Jewish and non-Jewish) that talked about the cause of what exists and the cause of life.

Mediterranean Thought Culture and the Introduction
During centuries of study and reflection, always with the goal of finding the key to the fullest happiness, the philosophers of the various peoples surrounding Israel recognized a fundamental distinction between spirit and matter. Spirit is best identified with what we know of mind and will, things that are incorruptible, and non-material. Material is best defined by what we know immediately by our senses, but also by what we call its corruptibility. There are many variations in the discipline of philosophy at the time of John's gospel, but basically the insight is that there must be an incorruptible and eternal being from which emanates or proceeds a lesser

being, from which being there proceeds a still lesser being, and so on, each being always in some way and to some degree reflecting the first or original being, and yet drawing ever closer to the creation of what is sensed and what is corruptible. This continual emanation ends in spirit inhabiting matter, and there we find our world, a world of fleeting perfection and a world of corruption and death.

For pagan philosophy, the goal of the this-world existence of ours is to shuck off the material and corruptible so as to return and be absorbed into the original being and so become eternal and perfect, to the degree that this is possible. To know how to escape from corruption to perfection—this is wisdom. In this scheme, there can be identified lesser gods, until one reaches man, who is a combination of the spiritual and material. Thus man is at one and the same time one who is the spiritual image of the great god and yet one who is also enmeshed in the contradictions of corruptible matter. The way out of the morass of materiality is often considered to be "knowledge". If only I can know the truth of things, I can proceed confidently to separate myself from matter with the assurance that I am on the way to perfect incorruptibility. This knowing, of course, includes as its object the divine god and whatever that god reveals to be the sure way to free oneself from matter. One can see, then, that the divine god's word, which is the means of revelation, is crucial to saving oneself from corruption, that the word from god is what links one to knowing the god from which his spiritual nature, after many emanations, has proceeded into matter. This philosophical analysis of happiness was widespread and so had inevitably to be confronted by Christianity. Who is this word through whom I can free myself from corruption to live forever in imitation of the original god?

Jewish Thought Culture and the Introduction
But there is another way of looking at creation: it is the way of the Old Testament. Genesis records a story that rhythmically quotes the word of Israel's God, "Let it be…" and the result "…and so it was", and God called everything He made "good". In this way the Old Testament reminds its readers that the entire world is a result of God's speech, that God created through a "word". Thus, creation moves from God through His word to the reality created. Immediately we note: here there are no

emanations arriving at matter, nor is matter evil; matter is repeatedly called "good".

This particular analysis of creation is paired with another that can be seen as the second creation story of Genesis (Genesis 2, 4b – 3, 24). Here God is said to form man from dirt and then breathe into him that spirit or life which is not corruptible material. Here the life-giving God does not create by speech, but by touching and breathing.

In both of these Jewish explanations of the universe, all is to be understood as caused by God, as being good even though it is material. Man is said to be in the image and likeness of God, and this indicates that man's goal or reason-for-being is to become ever more perfectly the image and likeness of God. It is through this remaining in God's likeness that man overcomes the corruptibility of death and lives forever, like God. And it was because of sin, not because of matter itself, that man finally knows death.

Creation, in each of the Genesis creation stories, is similar to the insights of ancient philosophers in that both agree that the origin of the world lies in a great power from whom all creation comes, and that created human beings try to save themselves by returning to the great power to be "like it". And all agree that it is through wisdom that a human being can achieve freedom from corruption and death. For pagan philosophers, one studies to learn the wisdom needed for salvation from corruption. For Israel, wisdom is not reached by study but by obedience to the Law revealed to Moses. Thus Old Testament wisdom is distinct, both in content and in source, from the philosophies contemporaneous with it. At a definite point in time, certain inspired Old Testament writers spoke not only of the Mosaic Law as an expression of God's wisdom, but also of a "Lady Wisdom" who reflects the mind, the wisdom of God in His full creation. Thus, not just the Mosaic Law is an expression of the wise mind of God, but all creation as well. Because of the supreme importance of the Law given to Moses, Lady Wisdom contains this Law and so takes up her abode in Israel, the land of the Law. "Lady Wisdom" is not, in the Old Testament, a person; the term is a personification of the externalization of God's mind. That is, 'Lady Wisdom' is a poetic way of describing all that God speaks so as to create; she is supremely important in the created human being's attempt to find her, for it is through knowing "her", God's expressed thinking, especially His will which He expects to be obeyed, that the created human being will find Him and salvation. For philosophy and for the Old Testament, God cannot be said to have brought to creation all that He thinks. There is always the conviction that God's wisdom is infinite, and so is only partially revealed. Certainly He can reveal more than what human beings know at any one time. Thus, wisdom like God is known and unknown, all to the degree that God wishes. But it remains true to say that God can express His wisdom outside Himself (e.g., by creation or revelation), and so wisdom remains hidden until God speaks through His word, which is the expression of His wise mind.

It can be said that John's poem benefits from all this kind of reflection, pagan and Jewish. He likes particularly the fact that the way to gain happiness in pagan philosophies is through knowledge of a word which leads one back to its divine speaker, and he likes the fact that in Judaism the world reflects God who created by a word. In either case, the concept of "word" becomes the first crucial means of introducing John's central concern: to gain everlasting life. Through the word created human beings will find total happiness, for through the word they finally know the mind or wisdom of God. This word, a part of which is expressed in creation (and is therefore knowable from creation), will be "made flesh". Thus will human beings hear the word which leads to eternal life. In this way of thinking the word stands both as the means of creation and as the means of salvation, for as "word" it stands as the exteriorization of the mind of God, who creates and saves through His speech. But with John, the Word will no longer be a personification of a quality, but a Person who will still be the perfect reflection of the mind of the God who gives eternal life through His Word.

Characteristics of the Word

Most important for John is the first Genesis story (Genesis 1, 1 – 2, 4a) which explicitly tells us that God creates through His Word. This suggests to us that His Word has always been in God's mind and, as such, is God. A word when spoken can only reflect the mind of its speaker; it has no other content. And so it is with the Word of God: the Word has no other content than what is in the mind of God. Moreover, the Word lives as long as the Word is spoken, for God has spoken the Word which has no beginning or end. The Word has no other existence than that shared with the Speaker, for the Word has no existence independently of the Speaker, and so the Word lives by the very life of God. But there is an important difference between this Word and another "word". The Speaker of the Word is not His Word; He speaks this Word, which in turn is not to be confused with the Speaker. Indeed, the Speaker can exist without speaking, and continue to exist if He speaks no longer. Thus the Word is divine, for its life is the divine Speaker's life, and the Word is nothing other than the thought of the divine mind. On the other hand, there is no confusion between the Speaker and this Word—the distinction between the two is clear. In John's presentation, "the Word was with God" (thus, separation from God) and "the Word was God" (thus, identity with God).

John writes as a believer to believers. He wants them to understand the fundamental meaning of the person, Jesus, in whom they believe. For John at this moment of introduction, Jesus is the one through whom the wisdom of God passes into creation. Jesus is the one through whom all things God thought of and chose to speak of are made. Jesus is God's spoken Word-made-flesh. It is not enough at this point to say that Jesus is Messiah, Lord, Savior or any or all of the other titles applied to him. For John, the Word becomes flesh, he is the one through whom the entire world exists. As Word he reflects the mind of God and, once human, he reveals the mind of God. It is this creator of being who has become human in some forever mysterious way. In Jesus the man the Word takes on a new existence, a human existence, while never relinquishing His existence in God, for "the Word was God". Every time one looks at Jesus, then, one cannot help but think, in Johannine Christianity, that one is looking at a cause of the entire world, a cause which holds the universe in existence, for God has spoken "universe" through him who "was with God and was God" (Gen 1, 1).

Jesus as Life and Light

But John's introductory poem moves on from the formidable and profound explanation of the function of the Word God spoke (who eventually became a human being) as source of all creation. As noted earlier, John is above all concerned with pointing out the way to life everlasting, a life While the notion of life, and how to maintain it, is a concern of the Gentile philosophies, life in its fullness had for centuries been a central and defining value of the Old Testament. Indeed, most all of the Old Testament is a vigorous teaching of this one principle: if you obey, you will live; if you disobey, you will die. The Old Testament had defined the greatest punishment of disobedience to be death. The fullest and hoped-for life would be that in union with God who is life and lives fully forever. It is a union so intimate that we have no human terms to express it adequately. John now offers his first insight into the Word as the Word-made-flesh, who is Jesus. By virtue of this "being made flesh", the Word, the creative force of life, is known as Jesus of Nazareth. Life itself is its own witness to its indescribable worth. The life of Jesus of Nazareth is its own witness to its indescribable worth.

But when speaking of those seeking life, John is very clear that this life of the believer comes through "water and the Holy Spirit". With these words Jesus shows that his life-giving has the Holy Spirit of God as its means or catalyst; further, it is through baptism that God, through His Word-become-flesh, shares God's very Spirit with the baptized. To bring home the fullest significance of the Holy Spirit, we should recall that in human terms the life principle of God is the Spirit of God. It is, then, by virtue of our having God's Spirit that we share His very life and will live, like Him, forever.

John also makes use of another primary tool of the Old Testament—light. Many philosophies speak of "enlightenment". They are speaking about knowledge, the necessary requirement for happiness. In our daily language we too speak of "finally getting the point", an indication of the crucial step knowledge plays in our happiness. Woe, we often think, for those who "do not understand". The Old Testament, too, is consistent throughout in describing our way to happiness as involving "enlightenment". A particular image of light as union with the saving God is given in the Exodus story: all of Egypt was in total darkness, but light shone brilliantly over the people of Israel, and led the people through forty years of desert existence. Light is where God is, where life is. The unending affirmation of the Old Testament is that the Mosaic Law is a light to our feet, to guide us on a path to peace, a path otherwise unknown to us. Indeed, the primary quality of the pagan, who knows not the Lord, is that he is "in the dark". As with life, so with light: the great figure which will follow Jesus in teaching all that is necessary for eternal life is the Spirit, another paraclete (John 15, 26-27; 16, 7-15).

Paraclete is a word rich in meaning: comforter and consoler, judge, defender and personal attorney, teacher, giver of life. In every instance of its use in John, the word means to inspire the audience to continue to live in a life with God, in a life which will never end and which will always be in total light. If one recalls God's creative words "Let there be light" an "let there be life through my Spirit", one will realize that those creative words are part of the creating Word spoken by God to make all things exist. And this creating Word, through whom God bestows life and light, will then correctly be called "our Life, our Light".

John, having introduced the figure of Jesus as the source of everlasting life, now presents him as the light by which to see clearly who God is and what is needed to achieve life with God, for like God, we are made to live.

Life and Light in Human History
John then proceeds in his introduction to address history with the teachings he has just used. Light-and-Life, the Word who was to be made flesh, was in the world, created by the source of light and life, but the world, the pagan world, never discovered it. Given what is at stake in the finding of Life-and-Light, one can only commiserate with those who, as Luke says, "live in darkness and in the shadow of death" (Luke 1, 79) without hope of escape from eternal death. But also, within the people of Israel, those to whom life and light had been given through Moses and the prophets are a people, as their own history had shown, and they had regularly refused life and light. Likewise, Jesus himself, once he entered human history and exited it crucified, was not known by the world and was refused by his own people—he, the source of life and light.

As is typical of Johannine style, in John's poem a general negative (here: "everyone refused Jesus") is followed by an exception: "those who did accept him". These who accepted Jesus are John and his readers. Starting with the public life of Jesus, Jesus and his followers in the first century AD were consistently repudiated and often made to suffer for their belief in Jesus. The convictions of those against Jesus and his followers argue that these opponents do not have the way to eternal and perfect life. The Gospel is an extensive argument to the contrary: Jesus is the way to the truth which ends in the possession of Life, of God, forever.

Life and Light in John

To demonstrate that life comes through Jesus, John, after his introduction, offers seven signs throughout the first twelve gospel chapters. These are the change of water into wine (Chapter 2), the physical cures of the royal official's ill son and of the lame man at the pool of Bethesda (Chapters 4 and 5), the multiplication of loaves and the walking on the water (both in Chapter 6), the cure of the man born blind (Chapter 9), and the raising of Lazarus from the dead (Chapter 11). The very fact of such regularity in chapter spacing, always with regard to the theme of providing life for others, shows the power of Jesus, the Word-made-flesh, to give life and light. For John, Jesus' public life is a testimony to the life Jesus can give forever. A final sign, though not called such, is the death of Jesus. For those who can see, who are "enlightened" and believe, Jesus' death is, in John, the moment of Jesus' glory: "The hour has come for the Son of Man to be glorified…it was for this hour that I came" (12, 23-27). This is understood to mean that the death of Jesus is the clearest revelation of the mind which the Word reveals to us; it is a revelation of how much God loves us. Glory is not an independent being. Glory is a quality which results from valued possession, and the most worthwhile possession is the love of God manifested in such total giving as in the crucifixion. A time of suffering, yes, but a time of glory as well, for the value which deserves glory is "clearly seen" by those who believe.

The Love of God

It is noteworthy that all of these miracles, signs of a desire to give life, proceed from love. One of the strongest and most cherished statements of John is that of Jesus which measures and emphasizes the love of God for mankind: "God has loved the world so much as to give His only Son…. He did not send the Son into the world to condemn the world, but that the world might be saved through him" (John 3, 16-17).

Faith in Jesus As the Key

John recognizes that the key to possession of eternal life is faith in Jesus, for he the one from whom faith flows. This acceptance of Jesus and all he means is the door to all other benefits, e.g., the baptismal Spirit of God. This acceptance in faith enlightens one's journey to happiness: there can be no light if there is no acceptance. This faith gives power to become "children of God", perhaps the most revealing language for what it is like to be one who has accepted through Jesus God as Creator and Father. It is through faith in Jesus that one becomes a child of God. To become a child, one must be generated; here, the generation is consequent upon acceptance of Jesus, and through him of the Holy Spirit. Thus begins the distinction between "those who believe" and "those who do not believe", a distinction that resonated through all of the first century AD.

It is good to pause here to be clear about the development of John's poem up to this point. Jesus has been presented as the Word-made-flesh, the Word which reflects the mind of the One who speaks the Word. This Word shares, so to speak, in the existence of the Speaker. How could it be otherwise, for in our own experience we know our words exist only by virtue of their sharing our existence. Moreover, if God is the Truth, then the Word He speaks must contain the truth, for all the Word is the reflection of what God is thinking. Thus, if only a person hears the Word well, he has the truth, the truth which is in God's mind. Further, this Word is the means through whom the creator created the world. Thus, the Word existed before all creation and is its cause.

Jesus is the light by which one sees the Father, whom all long to see: "You have seen Him (14, 7c).... Whoever has seen me has seen the Father" (14, 9b). "...do you not believe that I am in the Father and the Father is in me?" (14, 10a).

Finally, the Word is the cause of what is, which means that whatever has life, has life through the Word. As the Word is the perfect reflection of what is in God's mind, so the Word, when God speaks It, is the cause of what God intends to exist and of what God intends to live. Life and truth are obtainable through, and only through, the Word.

Jesus as Son

Now John changes imagery. This change begins with the description of us, "we who believe", a term introduced only now at verses 14-18. And as a result of belief we are "children of God" (v. 12), again an image only recently introduced. A reason for this change may lie in the fact that now John wants to emphasize the reality of divine love, for Jesus is "filled with enduring love…. Of Jesus' fullness we have all had a share, love following upon love" (vv. 14 and 15). Indeed, even for Jesus the term "Word", so essential for describing the reality of Jesus, is replaced by "Son", the one who is most loved. From now on, Jesus will be called "Son of God", the most popular expression for Jesus in the rest of the gospel. After this poem John will no longer use "Word" for Jesus. It is not that John takes back what he had taught about Jesus as Word, Life and Light, but he will add to them and employ what is to him the most suitable term, Son of the Father, an appropriate title for him who will provide the reader with life forever.

As Son, Jesus is pictured as being in the "bosom" of his Father (v. 18), a place of intimacy and love. The languages serves as assurance that the Son knows the truth of his Father and, the Father being the source of all life, will share that life with his most beloved Son. Indeed, it is difficult to imagine one reaching the fullness of life in the Creator of all things, without faith in and without "passing through'" the Creator's Son, His Word, and His Wisdom. John's constant preferred phrase in his gospel is that Jesus is Son of God. Yet it is the image of Word which gives profound meaning to the title "Son of God", and was thought necessary to prepare us to understand most fully the identity and meaning of this Son who "rests in his Father's bosom".

God in Times Past and God Now

John completes the last stanza of his poem by a reference to Moses and use of the phrase "grace upon grace" (v. 17). Here, in somewhat cryptic terms, John refers to God's intense and historical involvement in the world. This involvement issued in the covenant with Abraham and his offspring and reached a climax in the formal covenant with the people of

Israel through God's instrument, Moses, at Mount Sinai. That covenant was a grace, a most beneficent act of the loving God, with eternal implications. John acknowledges that grace, but now points to a still greater grace, a much greater covenant, a much more intimate sharing of God's self with His creatures: it is not only His Law or promises that show His love, but the fact that the Father's Son has become one of us and will be the light and the truth to lead us to life. What the Law and the promises could do only in part, Jesus, the latest of God's graces or "the grace upon grace", will do fully. One must speak of death, a reality to be sure, but a child of God will live after death, for what else does Jesus "doing fully" mean if not giving life without end?

John the Baptist in the Introduction
Within his poem of introduction, John inserts some verses about John the Baptist. It is obvious from what we have already considered in Mark that no New Testament story of Jesus will begin without firm, clear reference to John. Indeed, one concludes, the divine intervention to bring people back to God began not with Jesus, but with John.

The Testimony of John the Baptist
One facet of John the Baptist we meet throughout the gospels is his role as preacher of repentance, a preacher sent to prepare Israel to meet its God in the final judgment or decision as to who will enter the eternal kingdom. In John's present poem this aspect of John is ignored. The e-vangelist concentrates on another function of John: to give testimony to Jesus. One way of describing this testimony is to say that John points to Jesus as Light of the world (v. 7), the Light which enlightens everyone to know God, to know Truth and so to have Life. At a second moment, the evangelist notes that the testimony of John points to the fact that Jesus is greater than John simply on the grounds that Jesus existed before him, a reminder to the reader that the Word was with God and was God "in the beginning", and has now taken on flesh to be Jesus of Nazareth.

Thus, John's testimony takes up the major part of the introduction: John points to the Light, the source of Life, the Truth. He states that "this one lived before me", which serves as a reminder that the Word-become-flesh existed before all creation. Jesus may have been born after John (v. 15), but the time of that birth does not give any hint as to the fullest reali-

ty of Jesus: he is the Word-become-flesh who existed before every created thing.

If one grasps well what John has written in his first eighteen verses,
one is prepared to listen to the story of Jesus' public life and to interpret it
properly and profitably. Surely it is easy to see how the people in Jesus'
public life did not comprehend at their moment in time the profound
meaning John offers us. Indeed, John's introduction prepares one to interpret properly the marvelous acts of life-giving and enlightenment that will
dominate the telling of Jesus' public life. In the light of the introduction
the reader is in the enviable position of understanding every moment of
Jesus' life as the life of the Word-made-flesh, the cause of creation, the
reflection of the truth that is God, the One who leads to undying life, but
also the Son who, while on earth, has not given up at all his presence in
the intimacy of his Father's bosom.

Hints of Conflict in the Introduction

Exalted as is this poem, it serves also as a comment on certain historical
matters. The poem indicates that the world did not know the Word, even
though the Word was in the world (v. 10). This is a reference, typical of
the Old Testament perception of the world, to the fact that the Gentile
world sensed the presence of the true God, but never knew Him. The
Gentiles by definition worshipped false gods; they were continually in the
dark, without light or truth. As Paul says, they groped to find the true
meaning of life, but never knew the Lord and so never found the object of
their unending search (Acts 17, 27). On the other hand, the Old Testament
typically insists that Israel believes it has always known the true God and
His will, which was expressed in the Mosaic Law. Further, Israel also
knows that it could not keep that Law and do what God wanted it to do in
order to enter unending life with Him (v. 11). Such then, is the picture,
much as Paul describes it too, of the world made up of Jew and non-Jew
or Gentile (cf. Romans 1–3). It is the entry of Jesus into this world and his
invitation to have the faith in him that now offers to those who believe the
opportunity to be nothing less than "children of God". One can see that
faith indicates the step one must take to cross over what seems so often an
insuperable chasm—to go from darkness to light, from ignorance to truth,
from death to life, from hatred to love.

Historical Circumstances

The historical setting of John's gospel, in which Jesus is in constant tension with those Jews who do not believe in him, reflects the historical setting of most of the first century AD Christian struggles; in Peter's words, "...realizing that the brotherhood of believers is undergoing the same sufferings (as you) throughout the world" (I Peter 5, 9). If, as scholars say, the John's gospel that we have is the final editing and reworking of a writing which was begun decades earlier by the apostle John—if that be the case, we note that, not only in the text we now have, but through every stage of its development, there is recorded a significant degree of conflict between Jesus and certain Jews. In the present state of the gospel, Jesus' remarks are often acerbic and harshly critical of his opponents, more so than in Mark or Luke. The reason for this continued report of Jesus' struggle with certain Jews is that the audience to whom the gospel, in its origins and in its present state, is directed has been under constant criticism and often attack by Jews through the decades since the time of Jesus. Basically, John's gospel is an attempt to argue, through the words and deeds of Jesus, that Christian Jews, a minority among Jews, are correct and true to God, and that unbelieving and belligerent Jews, who are in the majority in the Jewish Mediterranean community, are wrong. To argue his point, John has presented in his introduction to the public life of Jesus a figure who cannot be doubted to be the presence of the divine, for he is the Word who was with God and was God. Against this background of Jesus as Word John is confident that the objections of the non-believing Jew lose their force. John's gospel is a profound revelation of the identity of Jesus. Against a threatening majority it offers consolation and encouragement to the minority Christian Jews of the first century AD.

Faith and the Introduction

One of the elements in this poem of introduction is worth mentioning a second time. The poem makes reference to the fact that "all who did accept Jesus were empowered to be children of God" (v. 12). The acceptance of Jesus is identified as faith; one accepts him as the Son of the Father, and as the Messiah, as well. What helps one to believe are the miracles of Jesus, but one must be able to see them as more than just cures: for the one who can see rightly, they reveal the presence of God-with-us. Because of these actions or signs, Jesus expects the reader to understand that "the Father and I are one". If one believes, one is called "born from heaven". Such a one has the presence of God's Spirit and enjoys the wisdom and the empowerment to understand Jesus and God.

Without faith, that is without accepting Jesus as Jesus wishes to be accepted, one cannot understand Jesus, nor, John insists, God. All perception and knowledge of the divine things flows from the act of faith, which is an act based on reason as far as reason can go, agrees that one accepts a claim as true. Once one has accepted the claim, one is born again through the power of the One who has been accepted, one lives with God, enjoys His Spirit, and the food of life, one sees properly, and one will live forever with God. Thus, for John, "those who did not accept him" (v. 11) will not enjoy the benefits that flow from the stand one has taken by believing. This gulf between the believer, the empowered child of God, and the non-believer is a major affirmation about the world as seen by John's gospel. Perhaps John's is the most striking of the gospels for its separation of those begotten by flesh and those begotten by Spirit (3, 6).

Conclusion

John's gospel, then, hopes to be a means by which one believes ever more completely that "Jesus is Messiah, the Son of God, so that the reader may have life". Possession of Jesus means assurance of life forever, for he is the Word whose existence is divine and who causes all life to be. This person's love is unending, eternal, and so will bring those who love him, as love will do, to perfect and everlasting life. He is the Son, and so reflects perfectly the Father; he is the wisdom and love that are characteristic of the Father. If creation is a circle in which one begins from the creator only to return to Him, if the human person is completely happy and fulfilled only when absorbed as thoroughly as possible into the creator, the creator must show the creature the way, the truth so as to have life (cf. 14,6). God did this by having the Word, the Son, become flesh and dwell among us. Our possession of God and His possession of us, means that we must be possessed by Jesus, in whom we have all faith. It is through him, the Father has decided, that we will have the fullness of life with God forever.

John's Introduction in Context

Once John has given his reader a guide for his meeting with Jesus in his gospel, he describes the public life of Jesus in two stages: chapters 1, 19 – 11, 57 and chapters 12, 1 – 21, 25 (i.e., the end of the gospel).

The First Stage of the Gospel: 1, 19 – 11, 57

The first stage of the story opens, as we might expect, with a witness to Jesus by John the Baptist. Jesus is referred to here as Lamb of God, after the fashion of an animal used in sacrifice to make up for the sins of humans. In denying that he is the Messiah John leaves the door open for indicating who the Messiah is the one coming who is "greater than I" and the one "upon whom I saw the Spirit of God descend and remain". This one is the "Son of God". This witness of John corresponds to the introduction of the gospel, where the evangelist notes that Jesus is the only Son of God, who rests in the bosom of his Father (1, 18).

John, like Mark, adds stories about Jesus' calling people to follow him. These persons will become eye-witnesses of Jesus' major deeds and words. These calls culminate in Nathaniel's statement: "You are the Son of God, the king of Israel" (1, 49). Thus the Baptist and Nathaniel begin to profess, as a result of their experiences, what John has revealed in his introduction.

This first half of John's gospel reports seven signs, each of which expresses the fact that Jesus is the source of life and light. John had already said of the Word of God: "He is Life; as Life he is the Light of mankind" (1, 4). And John concludes his gospel with the hope that what he has written will help the reader to believe that Jesus is Messiah and Son of God and so the reader will have eternal life (20, 31). Do these seven signs perform their task well?

The Seven Signs and the Introduction

The first sign is the abundance of water changed into wine. The story emphasizes the power and willingness of Jesus to provide happiness to the full. Added to this sign is the notice, in dialogue form, that this "fullness" from the Messiah, the fullness of life and light, will be bestowed only after "I pass through my hour which is to come". Thus, though Jesus performs a miracle which makes us mindful of the benefits to be bestowed by the Messiah, we are cautioned in this sign that these benefits will come only after Jesus has passed through his "hour", i.e., his death and glorification.

The second sign is the healing of an official's son who was at the point of death. Jesus says to the father, "Go, your son will live" (4, 50). Then the servants come to say that "Your son lives" (4, 51). Here is another example which anticipates Jesus' giving life eternal.

The third sign is another healing, this time of a lame man who was unable to reach waters that would heal him (5, 1-9). If one knows how to understand this miracle, it becomes a sign that "My Father works still, and I do too" (5, 17). Jesus' opponents understood very well that Jesus was calling God his Father, thus making himself the equal of God. Can one read the miracle that way? Can one see how the miracle is also a sign of restoration that will be completed with the fullness of life?

The fourth and fifth signs occur in Chapter 6. First, there is the miraculous multiplication of bread, more than enough to feed all who wanted it. The food sustains life, and so Jesus once again shows his power to give life. Indeed, his is the only miraculous bread that assures eternal life, the bread that is his body. The bread which fed Israel through its journey through the desert was marvelous, but it gave no one eternal life. Then, there is a mysterious story of Jesus walking on water. Even in a gospel known for its rich use of symbols, this story holds out the symbols of roiling water as the symbol of death, from which Jesus now saves his church and one day will lead his disciples from death to life.

The sixth sign is a cure of a man born blind. The greatness of this miracle is appreciated when the cured man says, "From the beginning of time it was unheard of that someone opened the eyes of a person who was born blind" (9, 32). This physical miracle underlines the power of Jesus which will one day enlighten all of creation. It is Jesus now through whom this man sees. Jesus has been presented as the Light, the Light which is Life.

The seventh and final sign is that of the raising of Lazarus from the dead. At the words of Jesus, John tells us, "the dead man, still wrapped in the burial cloths—the dead man came forth from his tomb" (11, 44). This is the culminating sign, for it shows most clearly that Jesus is the one who gives life. Here we speak of a return to normal life where, we realize, Lazarus would die again. But the sign is to be read: here is the One who gives eternal life.

The introduction of John's gospel has organized the reader's thoughts before he embarks on a reading of these seven signs. From that introduction the reader anticipates a story about life and about light, Son of the Father. These seven signs play out these introductory themes and are designed to assure the reader that Jesus is, in truth, the one to bring all people to eternal life and light.

The Seven Signs and the Seven Discourses
But there is another element of these first twelve chapters that is important. I refer to the speeches, often dialogues, which John intermingles among these seven signs. These discourses can also be numbered seven. They are the discourse to Nicodemus, the discourse to the Samaritan woman, the discourse about the unity of the Father and His Son Jesus, the discourse about the life-giving bread from heaven, the double discourse about Jesus as Light and Jesus as the one who "was before Abraham", the discourse concerning the true shepherd.

Some of the most memorable words of all Scripture come from these discourses. For example: "God so loved the world that He gave His only Son in order that everyone who believes in him should not perish, but have eternal life" (3, 16); "...but whoever drinks the water I shall give will never thirst; the water I shall give will become in him a spring of water welling up to eternal life" (4, 14); "in all truth I tell you, whoever listens to my words, and believes in the one who sent me, has eternal life; without being brought to judgment such a person has already passed from death to life" (5, 24); "I am the bread of life. No one who comes to me will ever hunger; no one who believes in me will ever thirst (6, 34); "Jesus stood and cried out: 'Let anyone who is thirsty come to me!'" (7, 37); "If you continue in my word, you are truly my disciples, and you will know the truth, and the truth will set you free" (8, 31-32); "I am the good shepherd: the good shepherd lays down his life for his sheep" (10, 11); "I am the resurrection and the life; he who believes in me, though he die, yet shall he live, and everyone who lives and believes in me will never die. Do you believe this?" (11, 25-26).

The discourses of Jesus have become classic expressions of Christian life as he solemnly states that he will lead the believer past death to unending life. But there are two other aspects of this first half of the gospel that should be mentioned, beyond the signs and memorable words of Jesus.

Beyond Signs and Discourses:
First, it soon becomes plain in the public life of Jesus that Jesus is deeply concerned about his disciples. He tries to strengthen their perseverance, their continued faith in him. This effort in the gospel is a not-so-implicit statement to the readers of John's gospel in the 90s AD. Most scholars understand John's gospel as a call to Christians to remain faithful to the person to whom they had committed themselves, had committed their deepest hopes and longings. Mark's readers suffer for their faith, just as those of John suffer, as have many Christians before them. John's gospel is insistent that the believers are right to find in Jesus their one hope for eternal happiness.

It is also striking that John's gospel contains so little moral teaching from Jesus. Were we to have only John's gospel, we would not have the instructions of Jesus in Matthew and Luke—no parables, no wisdom a-bout conduct. The one commandment John offers is this statement of Jesus, "I give you a new commandment: love one another. As I have loved you, so you also should love one another" (13, 34). Of course, much of Jesus' teaching in the synoptics spells out what love of neighbor means in concrete situations. But what the gospel of John offers is the specification that love should be as thorough as that practiced by Jesus. It is not that one loves one's neighbor as oneself but that one loves that neighbor as Jesus loves that neighbor: such is the challenge to the Christian. The lack of specifics in morality in John's gospel only goes to illustrate three points. First, John's gospel is concerned about faith in Jesus and offers a view of Jesus designed to bolster that faith in as profound a way as possible. Second, the first two Letters of John respond to the lack of morality in the gospel with their own emphasis on love of neighbor. Third, we understand again why our New Testament is not made up of only one book or letter but twenty-seven: we need all twenty-seven to understand fully what God was about in Jesus.

Second, this first half of the gospel is filled with argumentation, especially bitter disputes in dialogue form. In this first half, Jesus clearly has enemies, those who will ultimately urge his death. John's gospel intends to bring forward the arguments and doubts of these enemies and to answer them fully. The concern in all this is the faith of the disciples: as in Jesus' time faith in him was challenged and put to the bitter test, so in succeeding generations, right up to John's time, there will be enemies, by far outnumbering the disciples, who will, by direct argument or by force or by ignoring the Christians, work to destroy faith in Jesus as the one source of life in its fullness.

A Summary of the First Stage of the Gospel: 1, 19 – 11, 57
John's introduction had prepared the way for the salient features of the first half of his gospel. One can consider these words:

> The Word was the real light that gives light to everyone;
> he was coming into the world.
> He was in the world, and though the world was made through him,
> the world did not recognize him.
> He came to his own and his own people did not accept him.
> But to those who did accept him he gave power to become children of
> God, to those who believe in his name, who were born…of God.
> And the Word became flesh and dwelt among us, and we have seen his
> glory, glory as of the only Son from the Father, full of grace and truth
>   (1, 9-14).

The Second Stage of the Gospel: 12, 1 – 21, 25
The first half of the gospel is concerned with Jesus' identity as revealed through his actions and through his statements about his relation to God. In the second half of the gospel we have eight chapters (and a chapter [21] added by someone other than John) dedicated to what Jesus said and did from his last supper, through his trial and crucifixion to his death and resurrection. The first half of the gospel covers almost three years of Jesus' public life; the second half covers at most a few days.

In these few days we might be surprised to find that John dedicates five chapters (13–17) to the last supper, the final evening of Jesus with his disciples. No synoptic gospel devotes more than half a chapter to the subject. Further, one of the most striking elements of John's gospel is his failure to mention as regards the supper any change of bread into the body of Christ, of wine into the blood of Christ. John is satisfied to omit this because he has already, in Chapter 6, identified Jesus as the Bread of Life (6, 34).

At the last supper, described more often by scholars as a "friendship meal" than a Passover meal, Jesus washes the feet of his disciples, like a slave. This story teaches two lessons—of an act of service and of an act of purificaton, i.e., a baptism that follows upon faith in Jesus. Throughout his gospel John stresses what the act is that corresponds to the reality of Jesus: faith in him. In this scene one is thoroughly cleansed if one is baptized. Peter, however, will fail at one point, and so needs a further cleansing beyond his baptism. At this last supper Jesus then predicts the betrayal by Judas (indeed, when Judas left, "It was night" [13, 31]) and the denial by Peter. Between these negative acts is placed the word of Jesus about love of others: "As I have loved you, so you should love one another" (13, 34).

What follows now is a lengthy discourse of Jesus which is, at heart, the things he wants to say to his closest friends and his future witnesses on the last night of his life with them. Various are the themes which make up this discourse, but they all point to the deepest meaning of Jesus, he who is the Word made flesh, Only Son of the Father, source of Life and Light. A major element of this discourse is Jesus' signal affirmation: "I am the Way, the Truth, and the Life" (14, 6). He is the way by which the truth about God and human existence can be found: and following him who is the Way one reaches eternal life. Another outstanding facet of this discourse is Jesus' attempt to show his intimate relationship with those who believe in him, the closeness of the vine to its branches. Where does a branch get and maintain its life? Thus, a human being will have unending life by remaining with its source, and the source is certain that it wants to remain with its branches, to give them life.

The Holy Spirit
Finally, Jesus introduces a new figure, that of the Holy Spirit. The Son is integral to the being of the Father, and the Spirit no less so. The Spirit had been mentioned as far back as 3, 5, when Jesus' talk was about life from being born from above, and in 7, 37-39, when Jesus clearly identifies the Spirit with that water which keeps one alive forever. In his last supper discourse Jesus refers to this person as a second Paraclete. "Paraclete" is a word for which there is no precise synonym in English; it means different

things in different contexts. This Spirit, under the title of Paraclete, is to teach, to console, to encourage, to communicate life and to defend. All this the Spirit Paraclete does. He is, remarkably, a second Paraclete; the first is no less than Jesus himself. As people believed in Jesus in his public life, so it is the Spirit who will continue to keep alive and vibrant belief in Jesus, a belief which continued from Jesus' own time till the days of John's gospel. Like Jesus, this Spirit is divine. It is a further expression of the supreme love which brought the Word to become human. One can say rightly that when this Spirit is given God has exhausted His inner self: the Father has given his Son and the Spirit. There is nothing left for Him to give.

As we have seen, in this discourse at the last supper Jesus constantly looks to the future, a future without his physical presence. What will happen to the disciples, and how will they react? Jesus foretells great suffering for those who believe in him; John's gospel is meant to strengthen believers under trial. Thus he offers words of consolation and encouragement. First, he speaks about his return: "A little while and you will not see me, but then in a little while you will see me again, and forever" (16, 19-21). Secondly, he speaks about his Father: Jesus' prayer to his Father will not go unheard, but will be answered: "that they may be one in us, Father." (17, 21).

This final speech of Jesus is of great value, something the other evangelists at most made only a small part of what they wrote. With this discourse finished, John now begins the traditional story of Jesus' betrayal, trial, death and resurrection. This story, like the speech, carries as a powerful undercurrent the knowledge that John gave to his reader in his introduction: watch him, the Word, the Son, in his final hours. Indeed, if the glory of the signs and discourses has made clear the identity of Jesus as Word and Son, then the humiliation of the Lord of majesty and the glory must also, somehow, help the reader to know Jesus as Word and Son.

Within the traditional story of betrayal in the garden there is no report of an agony. Rather, the story emphasizes the lordly nature of the one whose opponents have come to take to his death. If anything, this story teaches that Jesus went to death only when he gave his assent. He did not die because of being overwhelmed by greater forces. This story sets the tone for one of the author's main points in telling the further story of Jesus' trial. When Pilate said to him, "You will not speak to me? Do you not know that I have authority to release you and authority to crucify you?", Jesus answered him, "You would have no authority or power over me if it had not been given to you from above" (19, 10-11). It is ultimately divine authority, not human, which will decide Jesus' fate. Once again we see the harmony between the events of Jesus' public life and John's introduction which stresses the divinity of the Son that will be seen in all that Jesus says and does.

Jesus Messiah

A second important element in the trial, death and resurrection of Jesus centers on what can be termed a secondary title for Jesus in this gospel: the Messiah or King of Israel. Early on in the gospel, the subject of Jesus as king or Messiah (Christ) arose. "Could the authorities have realized that he is the Messiah?" (7, 26); "If you are the Messiah, tell us plainly" (10, 24). It is no wonder that the title "Christ" or "Messiah" should be the term about which Pilate should worry: he could overlook other, more in-house Jewish disputes, but he could not let pass a claim to be king (which is what Christ [Messiah] translates to for him). No such threat to Rome must be allowed to exist. An earlier statement by Martha, after the raising of her brother Lazarus from the dead, is very significant, for more than one reason. Martha said to Jesus, "Yes, Lord, I have come to believe that you are the Messiah (or Christ), the Son of God, the one who is coming into the world" (11, 27). Here we not only have an example of what would upset any Roman governor, but we also have the words with which John will close out his Gospel: "...so that you believe that Jesus is Messiah and Son of God..." (20, 31). Martha's statement also opens up the title Messiah (or Christ) to lead us to the further title: Son of God.

In introducing the title "Messiah" into the discussion of Jesus in this second half of the gospel, we called it a "secondary" title. Of course John knew that, for long, believers in Jesus were called Christians, a title which emphasizes the centrality of the title "Christ" in their faith. That the enemies of Jesus bring up this title in the presence of Pilate makes perfect sense. But, as Martha's words indicate, John looks on Jesus as more than simply the Messiah, no matter how much that person was longed for in Jewish hopes. John, we can say, goes more deeply into Jesus' identity, as his introduction already suggested. Jesus is the Word made flesh, the Word from all eternity through whom all things were made, and he is the only Son of the Father. If there be question as to whether Messiah means a person who is divine, there is no question about the divinity of the Word, only Son of the Father, who is Messiah. Some understood the belief that Jesus was Messiah to be a claim regarding an earthly king who planned to overthrow Rome and free his people. That understanding may have been plausible as Jesus' life progressed, but according to the final judgment of the gospels it was objectively false. Thus, John inserts into his gospel the title of Messiah, but he prefers to repeat, and repeat again and again, that Jesus is the Son of the Father, the Word that from the beginning was with God and was God.

The title Messiah leads to a more profound understanding (and definition of "Messiah") during Pilate's first interrogation of Jesus. Here, Pilate, having begun with the question, "Are you the King of the Jews?" (18, 33), brings forth Jesus' solemn response, "My kingdom is not of this world. If my kingdom were of this world, then my servants would be fighting so that I would not be handed over to the Jews; but as it is, my kingdom is not of this world" (18, 36). And when Pilate appears not to know the real charge the Sanhedrin has lodged against Jesus, the Jewish leaders make it clear, "We have a law, and according to that law he ought to die, because he made himself the Son of God" (19, 7). Such a claim goes far beyond the traditional expectation or definition of Messiah. Indeed, even a pagan would respond very cautiously and carefully, once he learns "the gods" are involved here. Thus, while kingship is a pretext for judgment before Pilate, and indeed such was the given, public reason for the crucifixion posted near the top of Jesus' cross ("Jesus of Nazareth, the King of the Jews" [19, 19]), John has emphasized throughout his account of the trial that Jesus is best and most fully known as Son of God, and is crucified as such.

The implicit message of John is that the reader see that the person crucified not simply as Messiah, but as the Word made flesh, the Son of the Father. This message helps explain the overall impression made in the Johannine story of the suffering and death of Jesus. John offers the reader two important guides.

First, many words and gestures involved in the crucifixion and death of Jesus are symbolic. Is John's gospel any different in this regard from the synoptics? The answer is yes, he is quite different. Not that the synoptics do not know how to use symbolic language. But perhaps the best observation to make here is this: Whereas the reader does not enter into a synoptic gospel with the expectation that he must be ready to interpret them, that is exactly what the reader of John must do. Let us look at one example of Johannine symbolism. When Jesus speaks his second-to-last word, "I thirst", one might be inclined to think that Jesus is suffering from a thirst which is very much a part of crucifixion; he is simply saying what every crucified person feels. But most scholars for centuries have seen in these words, "I thirst", a look of Jesus towards the next stage of salvation, when he will begin to save the many souls (including the Johannine readers) for whom "he thirsts". One might remain content with the surface meaning of Jesus' words unless one is alert to the possibility John may be using a highly symbolic kind of language.

Second, during these trying hours, there is a sense that Jesus dominates, that is, it is the Lord who speaks and his suffering is that of a Person from another world. This literary way of presenting the suffering of Jesus, which began with John's removing the agony from the agony in the garden, reinforces the goal of the gospel by applying the introduction to the rest of Jesus' life: he is the Word, the Son of the Father, the revelation greater than that given to Moses. Jesus embodies the divine Word. As Israelites tried to guess who Jesus was, they consistently concluded that no one in Jewish history (e.g., Moses, Abraham, Elijah, David) was the equal of the figure who moved among them from Galilee to Jerusalem. One might wonder why Jesus is compared with Moses. This figure who stands before Pilate and hangs on the cross breaks with all known realities of Israel's past. He is obviously human. But just as obviously, in this gospel he is divine.

The Resurrection Stories
John's resurrection stories continue to highlight the divinity of Jesus. Mary Magdalene wanted to hold onto the risen Jesus and keep him just as she stayed near him in the days of his public life (20, 17). What disciple

would not want to do that? We are reminded of Peter's request when Jesus was transfigured in a way that should make us think of Jesus risen from the dead. At the sight of Jesus transfigured Peter said, "Rabbi, it is good for us to be here; let us make three tabernacles, one for You, and one for Moses, and one for Elijah" (Mark 9, 5). Peter's is another attempt to hold on to that Jesus who must ascend to his Father. In his encounter with Mary Magdalene we hear Jesus clearly make the distinction, that he must ascend "to my Father and to your Father" (John 20, 17). By the time John's gospel was written, Christians were long accustomed to consider themselves sons and daughters of their Father in heaven. What is unique to Jesus' words to Mary is that he distinguishes between "my Father" and "your Father", thus carrying through the theme John has insisted upon from his introduction: Jesus is the unique, only Son of the Father. We are sons and daughters by infusion of divine life at baptism; Jesus is Son by virtue of his being fully God, by having his entire being, as Word of God, totally shared with God.

The Gift of the Dying Jesus: the Spirit

The resurrection story that concludes the original part of John's gospel describes Jesus' appearance to his disciples. Here we have two statements of Jesus that are significant.

First, Jesus breathes on them the Holy Spirit. We are familiar with the outpouring of the Holy Spirit at Pentecost, some fifty days after the resurrection. In contrast, John associates that outpouring with the resurrected Jesus, and has the Spirit given (as with Luke's account in Acts 2, 33) by Jesus himself. It is Jesus who breathes out the Spirit. In Israelite tradition such a breathing was characteristic of God, so in John the gift of the Spirit indicates that Jesus has this divine function. The gift signals once more that Jesus is divine.

Second, Jesus joins with this gift of the Spirit the authority by which his disciples can forgive sins. Such an effect flows from the gift Jesus gives, forgiveness as the sure sign that God's re-creative Spirit is now dwelling in God's creature. In Pauline terms what was lost through sin is now restored through forgiveness and a renewal of living with God. In view of Jesus involvement in the gift of the Spirit, one is led to think that he is here not simply an intermediary between God and man, but that he stands behind other actions which are ultimately ascribed to God, and, as

Acts has it, ascribed to the Spirit. Acts has no difficulty speaking of "the Spirit of Jesus" (Acts of the Apostles 16, 7).

Thomas

Finally, and fittingly, we read of Thomas's final profession: "My Lord and my God!" (20, 28). Thomas heard the witness that Jesus had risen from the dead, but said he could not believe it unless he touched Jesus. Logically, once he was invited to touch Jesus, he should have said, "You are truly risen from the dead!" But he did not say that. Rather, he said that Jesus is "my Lord and my God". John gives the final assessment of Jesus to Thomas, the assessment which is most in harmony with the subsequent verses which conclude the entire Gospel: "...that you may believe that Jesus is Son of God and so believing live forever". Jesus is not only risen, he is rightly professed as Lord and God.

Faith

At this resurrection story of Thomas's belief, one is tempted to review the entire Johannine story and read again where the concept of "faith" appears. Faith is important for all Christian writers, but becomes central for John as Jesus, in this gospel, continually and unremittingly calls for belief in himself. This belief is not simply "trust"; rather it is a conviction of the identity of Jesus, Son of the Father. One should not be deceived by John's use of the phrase "...and they believed" in passages in his gospel. Often he means that people are beginning to perceive something of Jesus' true being. John knows very well that no disciple really believed fully who Jesus was until after his resurrection. But his disciples begin to "believe" something about him before his death. In this way, these first disciples become an encouragement to the reader, first to plumb the depths of Jesus' identity, and, second, to go beyond the comprehension of those who follow Jesus in his earthly life. For from the first page of the gospel, the reader knows that Jesus is divine, but he must ever deepen and keep alive his knowledge of who Jesus—*his* Jesus—is.

With Thomas' affirmation this leap to the fullest identity of Jesus, John can contentedly close his gospel. True there will later be added to the gospel two stories: one about the role of Peter in the future church, and another about the fate of the disciple John. But the words of Thomas are the ones meant to return us to the beginning, to the introduction: Jesus is the Word, the Son, and so "my God". Putting together the two halves of the gospel, we can feel confident that John's introduction is a wonderful summary of and introduction to the adult Jesus of Nazareth, offering the definitive insight that the one I follow is nothing less than God.

[Without offering excessive commentary about John's gospel, we still should note the reason why Jesus gives his sheep and lambs to Peter to feed and protect. The reason is not what we might call "truth", as in the case of Matthew's gospel when Peter is revealed as rock of the Church. The reason is love of Jesus. That is to say, besides knowledge of who Jesus is (gained only be revelation from God), there is love. The shepherd (this is the image Jesus uses here) loves his sheep and lambs so much that he will die for them; therefore, he will give them into the care only of someone who loves Jesus. If a person knows who Jesus is but does not love Jesus, Jesus will not entrust his lambs and sheep to that person. He will be the "hired man", who proves not to be a shepherd, whose sheep are not his own because at the sight of a wolf he will flee [John 10, 12]). The good shepherd lays down his life for his sheep (v. 11).]

Matthew

Matthew had read Mark, whose work was by now in existence some fifteen years before Matthew produced his own gospel. He understood and appreciated Mark's introduction: Jesus was true Messiah and faithful Son of God. But Matthew felt the need to expand on Mark's introduction because he wanted to go in a somewhat different direction. Matthew wished to fashion an introduction that would suit his own concerns. More concretely, Matthew wanted to present to his Jewish Christian readers a story about Jesus which, in great part, defended the rightness of belief in Jesus as the true fulfillment of the Jewish scriptures and hopes. In this way of telling Jesus' story Matthew hoped to give solid encouragement to his readers against the claims of non-believing Jews who virulently opposed belief in Jesus of Nazareth. So he included Messiah and Son of God within a series of stories that will give his reader still further insight into the person of Jesus whose public life will soon begin.

Matthew's Introduction

In this Matthean introduction we see woven together three themes which will appear in various stories and words of Jesus: Jesus as the fulfillment of the Jewish scriptures, Jesus as the King of Israel, Jesus as the crucified one. Encompassing it all is the teaching that shows that Jesus is truly Son of God. The introduction begins with a genealogy which shows Jesus to be the completion of the generations of God's chosen people which begins with Abraham. Then we hear heaven's own witness that Jesus is Savior, King, Lord and God-with-us. Finally, as Chapter 2 plays itself out, we are made aware, through the threat to the child, of the opposition that dogged the adult Jesus: this bitter childhood experience is designed to give consolation and courage to the Christian Jews who themselves now suffer persecution and opposition.

The Genealogy of Jesus

Matthew begins his introduction to his gospel by presenting the genealogy of Jesus. Evidently it was Matthew's plan to begin the story of Jesus by using a scripture technique which would show him to be fully Jewish. Matthew especially emphasizes that Jesus is the son of Abraham and the son of David (Matthew 1, 1). When we read the rest of Matthew's gospel, we see that this call to think of Jesus as the product of his ancestry is only one of the many, varied and often very subtle ways that Matthew, a master of Jewish teaching methods, uses to show Jesus' relationship to the meaning and hopes of the Old Testament. Far from isolating Jesus from Judaism, Matthew shows Jesus as the fulfillment and completion of the Old Testament hopes and longings and promises. He begins, then, with a look to the past, to Jesus' ancestors.

The beginning of Matthew's gospel is not content to give a simple naming of past ancestors. Yes, it is important to see Jesus as Jewish and this is done by noting his ancestry. But there is something else involved in this listing and that is the meaning Matthew finds in this series of ancestors. Let us look at the matter this way. The genealogy is repetitious (as is the case in so many Old Testament genealogies which are Matthew's models here) and of itself offers little room for sure interpretation of its meaning. Indeed, we cannot be sure that Matthew was able to identify with historical accuracy all of Jesus' ancestors given to us here. But Matthew guides our thought by the way he introduces and concludes the genealogy. It is to those two points, the beginning and the ending, verses 1 and 17, that we turn our attention. The genealogy Matthew presents may be a compilation of ancestors from a variety of incomplete sources. But there is no doubt that we find the hand and intention of Matthew in verses 1 and 17, as a reading of them indicates.

Of all the ancestors of Jesus, Matthew has chosen to underline two: Abraham and David, as Matthew's first verse states. Why did he pick out these two?

Matthew 1, 1: Abraham

Abraham is noted for the promise God made to him. To Abraham God said, "All peoples on earth will bless themselves in you" (Genesis 12, 3) and "all nations on earth will bless themselves by your descendants" (Genesis 22, 18). Now given that Matthew was writing some fifty years after Jesus' life on earth, and given that the faith in Jesus had spread throughout the entire Mediterranean basin to include Jew and Gentile, it is easy to see that the promise made to Abraham that all nations would bless themselves in his progeny was fulfilled in Jesus. It is through Jesus that the promise of blessings, made to Abraham on behalf of all peoples, was able to reach everyone. Matthew, then, wants his reader to know that the fulfillment of ancestral blessings for all peoples, promised to Abraham's offspring, lies in faith in Jesus.

At first glance, since Matthew is so obviously concerned about Jesus as fulfilling the promises for Abraham's physical descendants, the Gentiles seem excluded; such seems to be the message of the public life of Jesus as Matthew has presented it. Are they truly excluded from the promises made to Abraham? Does Jesus in Matthew's gospel, which is so totally Jewish, ever avert to a blessing that goes beyond Israel? Yes, he does. Matthew closes his gospel with these significant words of Jesus: "Go therefore, make disciples of all nations, baptizing them in the name of the Father and the Son and the Holy Spirit" (28, 19-20). During Jesus' public life Matthew spends all his storytelling time on Jesus' mission to Israel. Jesus himself insists, "I have been sent to the lost sheep of the house of Israel" (15, 24). But to close his gospel Matthew points to "all the nations" as the sheep to which Jesus now turns is attention. And to prepare for this final word of Jesus, Matthew offers a first word: to Abraham had been promised that all nations would be blessed in the name of his descendant. Thus the phrase "son of Abraham", points to the world beyond the public life of Jesus, indeed, to the world of Matthew's time. In this way, Matthew, right from the beginning of his introduction to Jesus, wants his audience to see itself as the completion of the promise made to Abraham and now fulfilled in Jesus' coming. He is the offspring, Matthew insists, who fulfills the promise made to Abraham about blessings for future Israelites, first of all to all Israel, the physical descendants of Abraham, but then to the Gentiles, too, the spiritual descendants of Abraham.

David

Among many other things, David is noted for a particular promise God made to him. David had, by a certain time, welded the twelve tribes of Israel into one monarchy, with himself as king. Once David had done this, he thought to himself that he now lived in a house of cedar, a wealthy man's house, but Israel's God still lived in a tent, as He did for forty years in the desert. It was time, David thought, to build a proper temple for Israel's Lord. But at a certain moment God intervened and revealed that he had no desire for such a temple, but that He did have a love for David and his offspring. Instead of wanting David to build a "house" for Himself (in Hebrew the word for "temple" is "house"), He would build a "house", that is, a dynasty, for David. Only the family of David was to rule over this kingdom of Israel: his descendant would rule forever and his kingdom would know no end (II Samuel 7, 1-17). Such was the love of God for David and his offspring.

Yet, soon the kingdom of David was divided in two; then both parts were conquered by foreign powers, with resulting wholesale exiles. So what of the promise made to David? Would Yahweh be faithful or not to this promise of His love? By calling Jesus "son of David" Matthew asks his reader to think of the adult Jesus precisely as that king of Israel, that son of David, who was to rule forever, and who was to provide for his people all the many blessings God intended to give through this king to His people.

Think then, Matthew asks of his readers, of Jesus as the fulfillment of the promise to Abraham, as the fulfillment of the promise made to David. Thus Jesus is introduced in Matthew's, even before he appears there, as the fulfillment of God's promises to his two outstanding and revered servants.

Matthew 1, 17

Matthew chose to close his presentation of Jesus' genealogy with his own observation—the total number of generations from Abraham to Joseph and Jesus is 42. Matthew notes this and divides 42 into 3 parts so as to get the number 14. He could have divided by 6, or by 7, or by 21 or by 2. But he chose to divide by the number 3 so as to have 14 generations in all. Why does he want the number 14? Why is this 14 notable? How does Matthew look at it? In Hebrew, the sign for a letter is also the sign for a number. For example, the letter "b" is also the sign of 2, and 2 is also the sign of the letter "b". For our purposes it is pertinent to note that the fourth letter of the Jewish alphabet ("d") can be read, as circumstances require, as "d" or as "4". Similarly, the 6th letter can be read either as "v" or as "6". Because the number 14 shows a combination of 4 and 6 and 4, which can be interchanged for D and V and D, the conclusion of many scholars is that Matthew wants his readers to read the number of Jesus' generations as letters of the alphabet, so that the number 14, read as the sum of 4, 6, and 4 becomes "DVD" or, with vowels, "David". Matthew's point is that even the generations, if read properly, show Jesus as the long-awaited Son of David. The implication is that all Jewish scripture speaks of Jesus. Whatever was promised to David, then, is fulfilled in his son, whom the Jewish Christian knows to be Jesus. There is no other who is Son of David but Jesus. And, we should add, such a complicated interpretation shows our author to be a specialist in the intricate ways of Jewish interpretation of his time.

This is admittedly (to our way of thinking) a strange reading of the genealogical link between David and Jesus, but meaningful to Matthew and his Jewish Christian audience. For an audience convinced that Jesus is the Messiah, promised by God to His people, every aspect of the Old Testament should be used to show that Jesus is the fulfillment of God's promises to His people. The Old Testament is common and holy ground to the Jewish Christian readers of Matthew's gospel and their opponents. If the Old Testament can show that Jesus is the fulfillment of Abraham and David, then the genealogy in all its aspects can help defend Jewish Christian faith in Jesus. And Matthew, throughout the gospel, but especially in the first two chapters as we shall see, sets himself the task of showing how Jesus is often the fulfillment of all hopes and desires expressed by Jesus' ancestors for their children. It is he whom they should recognize from their scriptures to be Messiah, for in him all Israel will be blessed in the greatest abundance.

Is Matthew pulling out all the stops when he asks his reader to note how the genealogy yields the name David? Again, this is the kind of thing first-century Jewish specialists in the interpretation of the Jewish scriptures did. It may appear bizarre, but that is so to us, not to them.

The Annunciation to Joseph

For Matthew, Joseph will be the main protagonist in his infancy stories; Luke, in contrast, will prefer Mary for this role.

As often happens in the first century, authors (historicity is not in question here) will formulate their stories of heavenly interventions into human lives by revelations given through dreams or heavenly visits, whether of God or of an angel. This way of speaking is used so that there is no doubt about the truth of what is revealed, or about the fact that what is revealed is not the product of human thinking or effort. It is God who brings about and assures the truth of this announcement about the future.

The statements of "the angel of the Lord" (a term usually meaning in the Old Testament God Himself) reveal two essential facts about Jesus. First, Jesus has been conceived through the power of the Holy Spirit. As the angel implies, the child is conceived without human male intervention. Second, this child will be called "Jesus", which basically means "God saves through the bearer of this name". Both of these facts play an essential role in the believer's identification of Jesus. Moreover, the rest of the gospel about Jesus will be understood only if one understands that Jesus is always divine (since produced by the Spirit of God) and that Jesus is defined by God as savior. This means that no matter what impresssion Jesus makes as an adult, whether of a prophet or of Elijah or even of the promised Messiah, the reader must know Jesus as divine and savior. To put it somewhat differently: "divine" describes Jesus' being, "savior" describes Jesus' fundamental action; these factors are crucial to Matthew's revelation about the being and activity of Jesus. Without the understanding Matthew offers his reader, one does not get much beyond those people, friend and enemy, who historically lived with the adult Jesus and made their imperfect assessments of him.

Matthew does not fail his reader; he underlines a virginity which can conceive a divine person and assures that it is a fulfillment of Old Testament prophecy. He cites with great effect the prophet Isaiah, "Behold, the virgin will be with child and bear a son, and they shall name him Emmanuel" (Isaiah 7, 14). In this citation are foretold both the virginity of Mary and the description or identity of Jesus as "God-with-us". The word of the Lord to Joseph brings to fulfillment the confident hope that God would one day have this Emmanuel visit His people. "Emmanu" in Hebrew means "with us", and "El" is the word for "God"; thus, this son of Mary, while bearing the name "Jesus", can be called, through the vocabulary of Isaiah, "With-us-is-God". Again, Matthew, using the Old Testament to advantage, clarifies the being of Jesus: he is divine, God-with-us, conceived not by human effort, but by the Spirit of God, the divine savior of Israel. Matthew has prepared his reader well to understand the story of Jesus' astounding adult life.

The Story of the Magi

By design, Matthew tells of an event that occurs probably in the second year of Jesus' existence. History has relished this Magi story of course, but reading it after the annunciation to Joseph should make us aware that Matthew has nothing to say about the actual date of the birth of Jesus. His story of the revelation of the angel of the Lord to Joseph occurred sometime when it was apparent that Mary was pregnant; the coming of the Wise Men occurs well after the birth of Jesus. Matthew has chosen, for his introduction, stories he finds meaningful about Jesus, and at the same time he does not wish to report on the actual birth of Jesus. Perhaps is disappointing, but the choice was Matthew's. Our observing what he did here only underlines a basic characteristic of gospel writing: the gospel writer is free to choose what stories he wishes to tell, what stories he thinks good for his audience. He thinks he does quite enough in giving us the annunciation to Joseph and the Magi story.

The Magi

A first clarification is that the Magi are not kings, but wise men. Not all wise men are equal in their abilities. These particular Magi, the best at their trade, are, not unexpectedly, taken into the service of a king, possibly as far to the east of Jerusalem as Babylon. Because they have discovered the meaning of a strange heavenly phenomenon they come as representatives of their king with gifts to Jesus, and they bring these gifts in conviction that they are coming to a king. What can we say about wise men of this era?

Wise men were professional students or "knowers". Their task in life was to know. Knowledge, then as now, is fundamental to human happiness, and so deserves the utmost effort. A wise man's whole life was dedicated to the pursuit of knowledge. The source of knowledge was "the earth and all above the earth and below it". The wise man searched everywhere he thought knowledge could be attained. There was no field of knowledge foreign to him, whether it was a study of a human being or the study of a society, whether it was a study of the heavens or a study of the underworld, whether it was a study of minerals or a study of money or a study of music. An important function of the best of a kingdom's wise men was that they counseled kings. Kings, responsible for the welfare of their peoples, needed desperately to know as much as they could in order to make the best judgments. Particularly they needed to know the future, and most particularly, the answers to such pressing and crucial questions as "Should we go to war or not?" The best of the wise men, then, would be found in the royal courts, advising kings from the knowledge they had amassed.

In light of this general description, our wise men are those who counseled a king that, from their study, they knew a new king was born to the west of them. Their knowledge came from their study of the heavens, where they saw a remarkable, indeed to them unique occurrence. In a part of the heavens associated with the land of Palestine on earth, there was a heavenly body that they had never seen before, a conjunction of planets which Matthew chooses to call "a star". That heavenly body was a sign, everyone on earth agreed, of a warrior and a king. Thus they concluded that in the land corresponding to this part of the heavens in which this event occurred, Palestine, there was newly born a warrior and king,

The wise men told their king of this new royal personage who had been signaled in the heavens. The reaction was immediate. As in our time kings and queens try to make alliances so that wars can be avoided and peace prevail, so this king made the effort to strike up an alliance with this newborn king. He did this by ordering some of his wise men to bring gifts to this new king and to show him reverence and good will. Thus the wise men of Matthew's story traveled from their home to reach this young king and honor him. As might be expected, they brought the best of royal gifts: gold, frankincense and myrrh. Gold is obvious as a great gift. Frankincense and myrrh are both highly expensive products of an intense and painstaking labor and the fruit of that labor are precious ointments from rare and faraway places. Only the very wealthy, the royalty, enjoyed these possessions; as gifts, they signal the great desire of the giver for peace and harmony with the receiver.

The Star

Matthew presents the heavenly body as a star. Matthew's star not only reveals but guides, for its function is precisely to bring the wise men to a particular house in Bethlehem in order to recognize in Jesus a king. Thus, the star first guides the wise men to Palestine, then to Bethlehem and finally to the house (not a cave) in which the Holy Family lives. When the star accomplishes its first role, to bring the wise men to Palestine, it no longer shone. Therefore the wise men went directly to the capital city, Jerusalem, because it was there that they could most likely find out "where is born the King of the Jews". Unfortunately, many years before this, Herod the Great had been designated by the superpower Rome as "King of the Jews". For the wise men to ask Herod where "the King of the Jews" was newly born was to threaten "him and all Jerusalem with him". The usual first-century BC reaction to such a question follows logically: the present "King of the Jews" will kill his opponent, the new "King of the Jews". So Herod consulted his own wise men, who are called scribes, those specialists in reading and interpreting the Jewish scriptures. They tell Herod that the precise town in which to find this child is Bethlehem. Again the Old Testament serves to illumine the story of Jesus: "And you, Bethlehem...no means the least...from you shall come a ruler who is to shepherd My people Israel" (Matt 2, 6; Micah 5, 1). One may be surprised that Matthew cites the prophet Micah and not such famous prophets as Isaiah or Jeremiah or Ezekiel. But this only indicates the breadth of Matthew's knowledge of the scriptures and that Jesus is witnessed to by all parts of the sacred writings, a proof in itself, Matthew thinks, that it is Jesus whom the scriptures foretold. So to Bethlehem the wise men go, again guided by the heavenly revelatory body. Herod urges them on, telling them to find the child, then return to him and tell him where the child is, "so that I too may go and adore".

As noted above, it is the opinion of some scholars that the "heavenly body" seen by the Magi was really a rare conjunction of planets. If so, Matthew would have changed this phenomenon into a star, and given the star characteristics of leading to Jerusalem and to Bethlehem and resting over the house of the Holy Family. Why this change? No doubt to make possible a reference to the prophecy of Balaam in Numbers 24, 17: "A star shall come forth from Jacob; a scepter (= king) shall rise from Israel". In this way Matthew has shown that the heavens, together with the Jewish scriptures, reveal the true meaning of Jesus.

Matthew ends his story with a few sentences about the Magi finding the child, giving him their gifts and reverencing him, then returning by another way to their country. Thus, the child is professed to be king and, by virtue of a dream, saved from the murderous machinations of Herod the Great. Matthew gives no indication that these wise men became believers in Jesus, or Christians. It is enough that they, pagans, give Jesus honor befitting his royal status, and that they, pagans, foreshadow the pagans who one day will actually believe in and follow Jesus. We should add that Matthew gives no number to the Magi; history has suggested they were anywhere from three to seven in number.

The first conclusion one draws from this Matthean story is that, as within Judaism there was expected a king called Messiah (or, in Greek, *Christos)* by whom Israel would be supremely blessed, so within the greater world there was born a king who was recognized as such and honored as such by pagans, and this was a foreshadowing of Jesus' eventual acceptance by Jew and Gentile alike. To son of Abraham and son of David and son of God and savior, our "God-with-us", we are to add "king" to the meaning of Jesus of Nazareth. Matthew feels we are almost ready now to read the public life of Jesus—almost, but not quite.

The Aftermath of the Magi's Departure
I use the word "its aftermath" to indicate that the brief vignettes that follow in Matthew's story all flow directly from the wise men's story, as if once the wise men begin their return journey, the effects of their involvement with Jesus end only with Joseph's bringing his family to Nazareth.

The wise men's story covers 12 verses; the three subsequent stories are respectively, 2 verses, 3 verses and 4 verses. Obviously Matthew has selected only the details that make his stories meaningful for him. The brevity of each of his stories also emphasizes the fact that all three, no matter how short, had to be associated with an Old Testament text. It is almost as if these stories are told primarily and in the first instance to show that the Old Testament, from its most disparate parts, witnesses to one person—Jesus.

At the departure of the wise men, God again speaks through a dream: Joseph should take his family to Egypt in advance of the coming of Herod the Great to kill Jesus in Bethlehem. Heaven protects Jesus of Nazareth. That descent into Egypt and the subsequent return to the Holy Land cannot help but recall to Jews that primordial and saving event, the return from Egypt of their suffering ancestors. So it is meaningful to Matthew to see in this journey of persecution the ancient and prophetic words that will reveal again who Jesus is: "Out of Egypt I called My Son" (Hosea 11, 1). The prophet Hosea had in mind that this "son called from Egypt" was the nation Israel. But, for Matthew using his rabbinic methodologies of interpretation the deeper meaning of the text, the divine meaning, is that this son from Egypt is Jesus.

The soldiers of Herod the Great arrive in Bethlehem. Not knowing exactly which small child was Jesus, they hardheartedly kill all the children they think fit the age given them by the wise men, i.e., those approximately two years old. (For scholars this means that Jesus was born about two years before the death of Herod the Great in 4 BC.) We would estimate that these children numbered thirty. Did anything justify this rampage? Only the fear that Herod and his people would be removed in favor of another king, and who in Herod's Jerusalem wanted that? Eventually, at moments throughout his public life, Jesus will have to make clear that he is not a king of this world, like other kings; his perfect kingdom is elsewhere.

The murder of these innocents reminds the sensitive Jew, Matthew, of another Old Testament text, now brought to fullest meaning. This text comes from Jeremiah (31, 15). The text is about Rachel, one of the four women who bore to Jacob his famous twelve sons, later called the twelve patriarchs, who are in turn followed, according to the New Testament, by the twelve apostles of Jesus. Rachel died in giving birth to Benjamin. According to custom the deceased was buried immediately, before sunset. Rachel died and was buried between Jerusalem and Bethlehem (according to one tradition), and so failed to reach Hebron where her husband and others (like Abraham and Sarah) were buried in the ancestral tomb. Many centuries later Jews of Jerusalem fled their city to Babylon or to Egypt as the Babylonian army took Jerusalem by force (586 BC), and transferred many Jews to Babylon. The prophet Jeremiah, one of those who witnessed this terrible conquest by Babylon, eventually fled to Egypt with others, and later poetically imagined Rachel in her tomb just south of Jerusalem and outside Bethlehem watching her children being forced from Jerusalem: she weeps, for her children are no more (Matt 2, 18).

Matthew now takes the same text of Jeremiah and applies it, not to Rachel's children exiled from Jerusalem, but to her later children, the innocents of Bethlehem whom she can see from her tomb: she weeps for them, for they are no more. Again, the Jewish scriptures have their role to play in making clear the meaning of events that are otherwise not fully understood.

About two years after Jesus was born, Herod the Great died. A successor to a large part of his kingdom was one of his sons, Herod Archelaus (all Herod's sons inherited their father's personal name, making of it their royal name). Herod Archelaus, we know from historical sources, was an unsuccessful ruler: he was cruel and totally uncompromising. Rome, who made all these appointments, always demanded three things from its appointees: money (taxes), men for the Roman army, and peace. Herod Archelaus could not deliver peace, and so Rome removed him about 6 AD, to replace him, not by other Herods, but by foreigners called governors subordinate to the legate in Syria. Pontius Pilate was one of these governors or procurators. (The legate was technically responsible for Palestine. Since he remained in the more important Syria, Rome appointed men, like Pilate, who acted "on behalf of" [pro] the principal "curator" or "caretaker".)

In light of these factors Joseph remained in Egypt until news reached Egypt that Herod the Great, who had sought the life of the child, was dead. Another piece of news was that Herod Archelaus, who had succeeded his father, had a reputation for hardheartedness and harshness. Joseph wanted none of that, and so, when he felt free to return to Palestine after the death of Herod the Great, he chose to avoid the territories governed by Archelaus and to live in a territory, Galilee, which was the top third of Palestine and was governed by another of Herod the Great's sons, Herod Antipas. (It is this Antipas who will behead John the Baptist and later judge Jesus at the request of Pilate [Luke 23, 8-12].) Thus Matthew notes, without giving us a clear reason, that Joseph chose to settle in a town called Nazareth in Galilee, the territory of Antipas. Because of that locale Jesus would be called "Jesus of Nazareth".

Matthew makes it seem that Nazareth, as a place to live, was a random choice of Joseph. But he also takes advantage of this obscure town's name to bring out another Old Testament reference (which scholars cannot find today): "He shall be called a Nazorean". Nazorean reminds the Jew of two possible meanings. A Nazir was a person who, perpetually or for a time, was dedicated to Yahweh. The word Nezer was a blossom on a tree limb. Nazareth makes one think naturally of both of these words, and each of them is applicable to Jesus. One who is the beautiful blossom on the tree of David, his father: "A shoot shall sprout from the stump of Jesse (David's father), and from his roots a bud shall blossom; the Spirit of the Lord shall rest upon him" (Isaiah 11, 1). Thus, Matthew makes into a significant choice what appears to have been a random decision: we will settle in Nazareth. Even the town gives deeper meaning to the identity of Jesus—if one knows one's Jewish scriptures and how to understand them.

Matthew has given his reader a profound understanding of the person of Jesus, the most amazing part of which is that he is "God-with-us", the savior. But another teaching to be learned from Matthew's introduction has to do not with a person but with a situation. Whereas the first chapter, i.e., the genealogy and revelation to Joseph, is free from any hint of the acrimony and death-dealing opposition that the adult Jesus will face, the second chapter with its account of the wise men and Herod the Great gives a clear miniature of the destiny of Jesus' adult life. In brief, we can learn here the terrible irony that, whereas those in Israel (Herod and all Jerusalem with him) opposed Jesus even to seeking his death, Gentiles, come to Jesus with reverence. Even the pagan recognizes him to be a source of peace. Matthew shows us that if we read the infancy of Jesus in the right way, we will see in it a prefiguring of the sorrow that will dominate the struggle of Jesus' adult life. In this contrast between natives and foreigners we anticipate the reality that, whereas the Jewish leadership will reject Jesus, so much of the Gentile world, particularly seen from the time of the gospel's composition, will commit itself to him in faith. The introduction functions as excellent preparation for the world soon to follow it.

Conclusion

Matthew reminds his reader of who Jesus is before he reads Matthew's version of Jesus' public life. That is, he asks his reader to remember always that Abraham will be the father of nations because through faith in his son Jesus the nations will receive the promises God made to Abraham. Jesus is son of Abraham. It is worth remembering Paul's argument, many years before Matthew wrote, that "if you belong to Christ, then you are Abraham's descendant, heirs according to the promise" (Gal 3, 29), for the true descendant of Abraham is Jesus and by extension those who have faith in Jesus.

Matthew also insists that Jesus throughout his adult life is the anointed one, the divinely promised son of the anointed David. Anointing is the moment when a person becomes king. Jesus will express in his life the wisdom, power and holiness of the Messiah or Anointed One. Jesus is son of David.

Matthew asks his reader to recognize Jesus as always king, the one through whom the benefits of God's kingdom can reach each and every human.

Matthew further asks his reader to realize that Jesus, throughout his public life, is Son of God. Whatever activity Jesus might engage in at any moment of his adult life, he is always Son of God by his very being. The conception of Jesus by a virgin and through the power of God's Spirit is forever a mystery. Matthew calls attention to the Spirit as a way of indicating that the power which brought Jesus to exist and dwell in the womb of Mary was divine. Since the Spirit is the divine cause, the child who is the effect of that cause is divine. Thus, though one can argue that Jesus must be divine because he has divine powers, one has a more thorough and all-embracing argument in Jesus' very being as the result of divine creation in the womb of Mary. No human being brought Jesus into existence. Divine the cause, divine the effect, and in this case the person of Jesus was conceived by a virgin. Jesus is Son of God and has no human father. As such, we can call him "God-with-us".

Significant for any reader of Matthew is the designation of Jesus as savior; his very name suggests this role ("Jesus" in Hebrew means "God saves through the bearer of this name"). From the way in which Matthew presents Jesus in his introduction, we will understand better the Jesus who saves by teaching the true wisdom of God through the sermon on the mount (Chapters 5–7), through missionary instructions (Chapter 10), through parables (especially Chapter 13), through instructions to his community (Chapter 18) and through preaching witnesses and the preparation for the end of this world and final judgment (Chapters 23–25). Matthew's introduction explains the immense power Jesus shows in difficult situations. In this introduction the evident love of Jesus for all, sinner as well as disciple, is seen as rooted in his divinity. It is the love which one has seen in past acts of the Lord.

Finally, this introduction, if kept in mind, will help the reader attach a positive, salvific meaning to the death and resurrection of one called Jesus and "God-with-us". At the last supper Jesus changes bread and wine into his body and blood, under the image of his terrible suffering of the next morning and afternoon for the forgiveness of sins (Matthew 26, 26-28). Too, understanding the role of Jesus as king and savior of Israel until Israel refuses him helps the reader to understand why Jesus eventually told his disciples to "go, make disciples of all the nations" (Matthew 28, 19).

As was the case with John's gospel, so with Matthew's: the gospel is written to encourage Christian Jews, a minority, to remain faithful to their convictions against the majority which is made up of many non-believing and oppressive Jews. Indeed, Matthew's first audience, the Jewish Christian reader, can renew his faith as he faces vigorous and painful opposition. Contrary to the majority opinion of the non-Christian Jews, the disciple of Jesus with Matthew's gospel grows ever surer of the person to whom he has committed himself. Because the Old Testament means so much to Jews and because Matthew makes so much of the Old Testament witness to Jesus, the Jewish Christian reader of Matthew has a much firmer understanding that it is truly Jesus about whom the Old Testament spoke, that it is truly Jesus who is the fulfillment and completion of Old Testament hopes and promises and the true interpreter of its wisdom. Opposition to Jesus, refusal to believe in him, crumbles as it is confronted with the Matthean story of Jesus, particularly through the insights contained in Matthew's introduction. Matthew's gospel is clearly a response in difficult times from a Christian Jew to non-Christian Jews for the benefit of Jewish Christians of the 80s AD.

Matthew's Introduction in Context

Once we leave Matthew's introduction, i.e., his first two chapters, we meet with a presentation of John the Baptist and of Jesus' baptismal experience and his private victory over temptations. And, once these stories have been completed, Matthew moves to the public life of Jesus and follows that life, at his own pace, till death and resurrection.

Matthew and Mark

Matthew, with 28 chapters, is longer by almost 60% than Mark's Gospel, and so we must be aware that Matthew found many stories about Jesus elsewhere than in Mark's Gospel. More striking perhaps is the Matthean tendency to gather into lengthy speeches many of the sayings of Jesus originally dispersed throughout his public life—a form of presenting the words of Jesus quite different from that found in Mark. Arguably the most famous of these speeches is the sermon on the mountain, which lasts a full three chapters. One of the more subtle effects of this gathering of sayings into speeches is that the pace of Matthew's gospel is different from Mark's. In Mark, once the action starts, there is no end to it till death and resurrection: the speed of the story is notable. In Matthew, at least five major speeches of Jesus are so placed (chapters 5–7, 10, 13, 18, 24–25) that whatever speed may have accumulated comes to a stop: one settles down at regular intervals to hear Jesus' teachings. This balance between actions and speeches is intentional, and shows how different an author Matthew is from Mark, and how an evangelist can present the story of Jesus' public life as he wishes.

Four Matthean Themes

We saw in Matthew's two-chapter introduction these four themes: 1) Jesus as divine Son of God, which merits him the title "God-with-us"; 2) Jesus as descendant-inheritor of Abraham and David; 3) Jesus as king of Israel who is treated like a king by pagans; 4) Jesus as one destined to be persecuted. All of these themes are wrapped, so to speak, with the pages of the Old Testament. Let us see how these themes play out in the public account of Jesus' life; we shall see that Matthew has written an excellent introduction by which he explains in advance his understanding of Jesus.

Matthew and the Old Testament

A characteristic element of Matthew's way of presenting the public life of Jesus is the influence of the Old Testament. The other gospels all use the Old Testament as a means of interpretation of Jesus, but none equals that of Matthew. For Matthew, who writes to Jewish Christians virulently opposed by Jewish non-Christians, the Old Testament becomes a common ground which both sides understand and revere. The argument, in short, is that if Jesus fulfills the Old Testament, he is deserving of belief. Jewish Christians did not abandon the Old Testament by believing in Jesus; rather they integrated the two. The Old Testament had a supreme importance for Matthew's audience: it was the word of God and one had a right to expect that the new intervention of God into the Jewish world should be in complete harmony with this basis of all life. While it is true that certain beliefs of the Christians are hard to find in the Old Testament (e.g., the Trinity, Jesus as divine, virginity of Mary), the genius of people like Matthew showed how these beliefs do not negate the value of the Old Testament, but in a variety of ways are in harmony with it.

The John the Baptist Story As Used in Matthew

As mentioned earlier, Matthew begins the story of Jesus with reference to John the Baptist. The Baptist plays two roles in his brief appearance in Matthew's gospel. First, he is a preacher of repentance, in anticipation of the continued preaching of Jesus about repentance. Repentance and the forgiveness of sins are fundamental characteristics of this new coming of God to His people. Second, not only does John prefigure the basic preaching of Jesus, but he also tells his audience about someone coming who is greater than he. John describes himself as one baptizing with water; that is, engaging in a ceremony wherein the baptized admits publicly his sinfulness and hope for forgiveness from God. Jesus, John says, will baptize the repentant with the Holy Spirit of God and not with fire. This means that he will use not fire but an indwelling Holy Spirit for the purification of the sinner's conscience. Most importantly, John does not have the power or authority to give God's Spirit to anyone. Only Jesus has the authority and power to give this divine Spirit to whomever he chooses. After all, Jesus is "God-with-us", and so can share the Spirit of God. The Baptist's witness, then, fleshes out the purpose of the savior, "God-with-us". John was highly revered by the people, and so his witness carries great weight.

Further, John was never a follower of Jesus and so is a strong argument in favor of belief in Jesus, for he had nothing to gain from his witness. His witness is, therefore, even, more believable.

The Temptations of Jesus in Matthew
Moreover, in Matthew's gospel, as contrasted with Mark's, Jesus faces three specific temptations in anticipation of his public life. Through his answers to these temptations he makes clear that his whole public life will be guided by what he says now to Satan. It is Matthew's intention here to help the reader understand Jesus' continual motivation throughout his public life, and then to help the reader adopt this mindset for himself. First, Jesus believes that life, the fullness of life, comes only from the word of God; he depends on something other than the things of the earth for his life (these earthly things are summed up in "bread"): only the word of God will give eternal life. He will listen for this word and obey it, for it alone will enable him to live. It is by doing this word that he will rise to eternal life. Second, Jesus has absolute trust in God, and so feels no need ever to ask God for a proof of His love for Jesus. Third, for Jesus there is only one God; thus, neither Satan nor anyone else will Jesus adore: he will love others, many others, but none other than God will he adore. No wonder that God can give public witness to Jesus: "This is My Son, My beloved; on him My favor rests".

Given what we know Jesus' attitude to be in the essential things of life, we are ready to follow him through a ministry which is governed by Jesus' basic beliefs.

The Public Life
Having shown that Jesus' appearance in the north of Israel fulfills an expectation, written in the Old Testament, that "from the north would come a great light", Jesus gathers to himself his first disciples,. In this portrayal of the call of Jesus to the disciples Matthew takes Mark's story of these calls as his own. Thereafter we are given an initial but powerful description (called a "summary") of the healing and preaching activity of Jesus on behalf of his people. Indeed, one can only be impressed by the power of Jesus over the most powerful forces meant to destroy mankind, and his good will to save people from their troubles. But then this action ceases

for a moment and we prepare ourselves for the first of Jesus' numerous discourses in this gospel. At this point in the story Matthew recounts to us the famous sermon on the mount. It is not our goal to analyze this discourse in detail, but we do want to look at what it might contribute to our belief that it reflects the introduction of the gospel and is prepared for by that introduction.

The Sermon on the Mount
Above all, one cannot miss the aura of authority that fills this entire sermon. It can only be likened to the giving of the divine Law on Mount Sinai to the Jewish people. But the giving of the new Law of God in Matthew is done both with the authority of God and with the authority of Jesus. The atmosphere of authority makes one think of divinity: this is not simply a human being (e.g., a prophet, even another Moses) who speaks on behalf of God, but one who, in authority, is fully comparable to God Himself.

As noted earlier, Jesus clearly distances himself from all other authoritative interpretations of the divine will: Matthew expresses this uniqueness of Jesus in the rhythmic repetition of the phrase, "You have heard it said (by your interpreters)...but I say to you". Let us also recall that Jesus ends the speech with a reference to "my words". To build a life on "my words" assures eternal life; one cannot say such a thing if one builds a life on the words of a teacher who is merely human when "my words" are uttered in contrast to the Mosaic Law. This affirmation is Jesus' final teaching on the mountain top, and so says that all the previous teaching of Jesus in this sermon is the sure way to salvation: all else is summed up in this small phrase: "in my words". One can see, behind this small phrase, the strong suggestion that "my words" are nothing less than "God's words". This divine authority of Jesus has already been prepared for by Matthew's' introduction: Jesus is "God-with-us".

One should note, in this sermon on the mount, the description of God as Father. The protectiveness, the love, the teaching, the guidance—these are all characteristics of "father" which Jesus wishes us to know as characteristics of God, "our Father" and "my Father".

A List of Miracles

Matthew's sense of order now prompts him to move from telling of lengthy speech to actions. Most of these actions of Jesus involve miracles, and, as in Mark's gospel, lead up to the central question, "Who do people say I am?.... Who do you say I am?" (16, 14-15). Perhaps there is a certain artificiality in these chapters (8 and 9)—miracle stories piled one on the other. It would be better to sort them out as surely as they were sorted out in Jesus' life. But orderliness is characteristic of Matthew, and placing miracles together has an advantage. Indeed, to place miracles together has a cumulative effect. Whatever one thinks of the historical accuracy from the standpoint of the time of occurrence of the miracles, in themselves they are impressive, and meant to be so: they are extraordinary actions of God alone, and they save, and they are in abundance.

The Second Major Discourse

Matthew interrupts the flow of activity in order to present a second major speech of Jesus: this has to do with the commissioning of the twelve and advice to them about their missionary lives (10, 1-42). It is not surprising that Matthew has gathered here the sayings of Jesus that affect missionary life at the time his gospel was written; in this way, Matthew makes contemporary words which had been spoken over fifty years before. Again, in this discourse one recognizes the authority of divinity and the foreknowledge that is divine. The influence of the Introduction continues, whether it be in terms of the divine mandate to witness to Jesus or the preparation of disciples for rejection.

The Increasing Opposition

As one now moves to a further recounting of Jesus' wonders and sayings, one cannot miss the growing opposition to Jesus: it will be the same opposition Jesus' followers will meet in Matthew's own time. Matthew tells the story of Jesus in such a way that his Jewish Christian readers will recognize their own precarious situation which is caused by a virulent rejection of anything to do with Jesus. In this Jewish atmosphere, one cannot but see the Christian Jew as the continuation of the prophets who were persecuted for their beliefs.

The Third Major Discourse

A third sermon (Chapter 13) asks us to listen to a series of parables from Jesus. These parables were given at different times in Jesus' public life rather than all at once in one speech as they appear in Matthew. Matthew organizes them into one sermon, and hopes thereby that each of the parables gains by association with the others. It is clear from the parables that the stakes are high: one is ready to give everything in order to have the kingdom of God. Jesus seems to look fixedly on the end of life: it is with this end of life in view that one makes one's choices now.

Bestowal of Grace and Responsibility on Peter

Opposition to Jesus grows on all sides, whether it be from his own town of Nazareth, or from religious leaders who claim he is a servant, not of God, but of Satan. Peter stands out from and above others, as he confesses that Jesus is the Messiah, the Son of the living God. Every gospel recalls this painful fact: the Peter who understands much about Jesus will deny him at the end. The story is a piece of history, but also a challenge to the reader: is he any different from Peter?

In Matthew's gospel, Peter can confess that Jesus is the Messiah of the living God because God gives him this revelation. Jesus recognizes the source of Peter's confession and using it as the basis affirms "on you, Peter, I will build my church". Moreover, there follows from this cardinal role of Peter that whatever he forgives will be forgiven by God. How does Jesus know to give this singular privilege to Peter? As Jesus says, "Flesh and blood (i.e., human reasoning alone) have not led you to conclude to my being Messiah of God, but you know it by virtue of a revelation from God". The perception of Jesus' identity is a gift from God. Jesus provided actions and sayings that would make sense of saying that Jesus is Messiah, but the actual leap to affirm this identity is necessarily a gift from God. Indeed, Peter confesses Jesus to be Messiah and Son of God. The introduction has already set the meanings of these two precious titles of Jesus. (Contrarily, in the other synoptics Peter's judgment that Jesus is Messiah is a human judgment based on human experience of Jesus.)

For us, one of the most important aspects of the story about Peter as rock of the church is, once again, the presence of the important pronouns, "I" and "my". Jesus affirms that it is he who will build the church on Peter, and this church will be "his church". One understands Jesus' words even better when one realizes that "church" is a word meaning a group who comes to listen to the word of God and worship Him—the Sinai event is the model of this kind of "church". At Sinai, one can call the children of Abraham assembled at the foot of the mountain "God's People". At this point in Matthew it is clear that the church, built by Jesus, will be "Jesus' Church". In saying this, Jesus is suggesting a quailty of Jesus that Matthew had given us in the introduction: Jesus, in having his own people, is divine.

Messiah

As was true in Mark's gospel, and will be true with Luke, to call Jesus Messiah, according to its traditional sense, is not enough. One reason is that no one, including Peter, thought that Messiah included crucifixion, even after his revelation from God about the identity of Jesus. This full truth about Jesus would only be understood and accepted after Jesus' resurrection. Speaking about morality, the way Jesus handled death is still to come, a way of submitting to the divine will of his Father that revealed how faithful to his Father was this Son; no one knew this till after the resurrection.

We recall that the word "Messiah", though etymologically meaning "anointed one", meant for many Jews of Jesus' time a king. There had been for so many centuries a longing for a world in which a king would rule in Israel who would free Israel from its enemies, and, through wisdom and power and devotion to the Lord, provide the greatest kingdom Israel would ever know. Given the activities and teaching and holiness of Jesus, it becomes clear that, in Jewish terms, he merits to be called king; indeed, over his cross it will say, "This is Jesus, the King of the Jews" (27, 37). Such was the written charge against Jesus as Pilate understood it. Such a regal presence throughout Jesus' public life only reminds us of the introduction of Matthew in which we were promised one whom even pagan wise men would worship. The public life lives out the introduction, which indicates the way in which Matthew wants his reader to interpret Jesus.

Two Final Discourses of Jesus

As we draw nearer to the close of Jesus' public life, we once again interrupt his life of teaching and good deeds to hear two discourses. First, there is the sermon in which he gives guidelines for how future community members should relate to each other (18, 1-35). In this sermon mercy is the primary quality, a mercy already expressed in the great and traditional Mosaic commandment, "You shall love others as you would love yourself". In the light of the introduction Jesus' teaching here is that of a divine being, reminiscent of the divinity which spoke similar words on Sinai.

Then, there is the lengthy sermon, concluding with parables, as regards the end of time and the judgment of the world (22–26). This sermon presents the role of Jesus at the end of this age: rather than God as judge of the world, as Jews believed, Jesus will be the judge. Thus Jesus again is the one who acts in accord with his identity, "God-with-us". There is no doubt of this when one reads, for instance, the last words of Jesus at the end of his public life.

It is the Son of Man, now in glory after his extreme humiliation, who will judge all, and the criterion for entering the Kingdom of "my Father" (26, 34) is how one has acted toward Jesus. "What you did for one of the least of people, you did for me" (26, 41). Moreover, it is just before this speech that Jesus delivers a bitter, sustained tirade against the Scribes and Pharisees who seek to destroy him. In this series of woes, Jesus mentions that after Jesus dies, animosity towards him will produce even the martyrdom of "prophets and wise men whom I will send to you". What were themes of the introduction, persecution and divinity, are now visible in the sufferings of his followers because of him and his claim that he, now rather than God, sends prophets and wise men to his people.

Jesus' Final Days in Jerusalem

There are four moments in the final part of Matthew's gospel that are particularly meaningful in modern terms. First, we have Jesus' entry into Jerusalem (21, 1-11). Second, Jesus pronounces words that change bread and wine into his body and blood (26, 26-30). Third, the agony Jesus suffered in the garden (26, 36-46). Fourth, the profession from the centurion at the cross (27, 54).

The Entry into Jerusalem

One recognizes in Jesus' entry into Jerusalem a momentous step in the Matthean story. The ordinary narrative of the words and deeds of Jesus, and of opposition to him, as well as good will—all this receives an emotional and exhilarating energy by the story of Jesus' very symbolic mode of entering that place about which he had said, "…we are going up to Jerusalem, and the Son of Man will be handed over…and they will condemn him to death, and hand him over to be crucified" (20, 18-19). It is at this point in the story that Matthew makes use of one of the many Old Testament texts he employs to show how the Old Testament spoke precisely about Jesus: "Say to daughter Zion [i.e., Jerusalem], 'Behold your king comes to you, meek and riding on an ass…'" (Zechariah 9, 9 and Matthew 21, 5). The harmony between the events of Jesus' life and the Jewish scriptures should help remove all hesitation to believe in Jesus. The Jewish scriptures, the Matthean argument goes, are the most satisfying explanation of Jesus' life. How can the non-believing Jewish community argue against that? Noteworthy too is the comparison: As with the Magi in their story in the introduction to his gospel, Matthew shows again with the crowds praising Jesus that Jesus is King.

The Words at the Last Supper
A second moment of interest to us are the words of Jesus at the last supper, those words by which he changes bread and wine into his body and blood. Put simply, could any prophet or even a Moses or an Abraham suggest that his body and blood could be received as food? Such a claim is divine, and another example of the introduction to Matthew's gospel, which affirms in no uncertain terms that Jesus is divine. Indeed, if there had been a liturgical ceremony involving blood to celebrate the covenant of Sinai, the blood of the new covenant would have been seen as its unique fulfillment. The new covenant is "eternal", i.e., definitively unique and hence united the two covenant partners in a definitively unique way which is destined to last forever. Such a unique covenant is appropriate for the uniquely human and divine Jesus. Moreover, this body and blood was for the forgiveness of sins. In the light of the introduction, this is God's own blood which works this divine gift of forgiveness. Ultimately, as food and drink, the body and blood of Christ is to be the strength of the Christian and the assurance of forgiveness and success in reaching eternal life.

The Agony in the Garden

We have discussed, in looking at Mark's gospel, the relationship between Jesus words during his agony in the garden and Mark's opening statement that said that Jesus is Son of God. Jesus' words stress not only his obedience in the face of undesired death, but also his awareness that he is Son of the Father whom he is anxious to obey. Again, we have a story infused with what we saw about divinity in the introduction. Matthew can only say that, in a mysterious way, it is God Himself who dies for the sins of mankind; the Son agreed to do what His Father asked.

The Centurion's Confession

Finally, another intentional indication that Jesus is divine is given through the words of the centurion and his men after Jesus' death: "Truly, this was the Son of God!" (27, 54). What is particularly meaningful here in Matthew's gospel is that the testimony to Jesus is by more than just the single centurion, and that they gave their witness to Jesus as a result of their extraordinary experience: "...they feared greatly when they had see the earthquake and all else that was happening" (27, 54). It is from that fear, so long associated in Jewish minds with fear of God, that comes the profession "Truly, this was the Son of God!" Luke has the centurion call Jesus "just" or "innocent"; Matthew, like Mark, prefers to call Jesus "Son of God". Matthew's change is determined by his desire that his readers see in the crucified Jesus a Son who perfectly obeyed his Father.

Words of the Risen Jesus

One final example of the presence of the introduction within the greater gospel story occurs at the very end of the gospel. Here the risen Jesus gathers his disciples for final words of farewell. Among these words is the promise that "I will be with you always, until the end of the age" (28, 30). A human being might make such a statement with a rather poetic touch: "even the grave cannot separate us, can keep us from loving each other". But from the earliest years of Christianity these words have been taken to mean that Jesus promises a real and active presence in the lives of the believers. How he will do this is not explained in Jesus' public life, but it follows clearly from the gospel's introduction, which revealed both his divinity and his love which brought him to be one with those for whom he died. No doubt Matthew felt that his readers would only confirm that they had known the presence of Jesus among them.

Moreover, in these final words of Jesus, there is a subtle reference that can be understood and appreciated by those who have been baptized and taught even though Matthew does not make the allusion to baptism explicit. Jesus says that baptism will be "in the name of the Father and of the Son and of the Holy Spirit" (28, 19). There can be only one identify-cation of these three persons: they include Jesus who is, however one explains it, the Son who shares the one name with the Father and the Son.

We have waited long for the introduction to be fully represented in the gospel; now that happens. In the final words of Jesus to his disciples, Jesus clearly directs his followers' attention to "all nations". Up until these final words Jesus, in Matthew, has been most insistent that he has been sent only to Israel. In comparing Matthew's gospel with the other three, it is clearest in this gospel that Jesus understands himself right up to his death as missioned by God to Israel. One of the most significant state-ments of Jesus in this regard is his reply to his disciples: "I was sent only to the lost sheep of the house of Israel" (15, 24). Luke and Mark have this story in their gospels, but do not emphasize, as Matthew does, this single-minded concern of Jesus for his own people. Thus it is noteworthy that when Jesus gives final instructions to his disciples they are that the disci-ples should go to all nations, baptizing and teaching them. The crucial turn of Jesus' thought to all nations occurs only after he dies. Right up to the end of his life, his interest is centered on Israel. Thus, in later years, especially in the time of controversy between Christian and non-Christian Jews, Matthew makes clear that Jesus felt his ministry was limited to Israel, and never decided to go to the gentiles until Israel had formally rejected him in the trial before Pilate. Such was the import of the words in which they, in place of Pilate, took responsibility for Jesus' death: "I am innocent of this man's blood. Look to it yourselves". And the whole people [i.e., those present] said in reply: "His blood be on us and on our children" (27, 24-25).

Finally, what in the introduction prepares us for this universal mission to "all nations" that we find in Matthew 28? The indicators in Matthew's introduction are two: the respect Matthew shows to the wise men and the mention of the name of Abraham.

Having mentioned the wise men a number of times elsewhere, we need here only stress that the heavy symbolism of the introduction story is finally to be realized. In Matthew's introduction we heard of the attempt to kill Jesus and of his acceptance by pagans. Now the implications of that story for the public life of Jesus have come true: certain Jewish authorities were instrumental in having Jesus crucified, and, as Matthew's community of the 80s AD can testify about the Mediterranean Christian communities, many pagans have accepted Jesus as their Lord.

The significance of Abraham is now clear. Matthew has shown the full meaning of the Messiah, the definitive son of David, in fulfillment (if one interprets correctly) of such texts as II Samuel 7, 12-13.16 and Isaiah 9, 7. This son of David would later be recognized as Messiah and king. Indeed, the entire gospel shows reasons why Jesus deserves to be considered this Son of David. But antedating the promise made to David, is the promise given to Abraham, that he would be the father of many nations (Genesis 17, 5) In him would all nations be blessed (Genesis 12, 3). Generations of the children of Abraham waited for centuries to have this promise fulfilled. Scholars think that the mention of Abraham at the very beginning of the gospel is Matthew's way of alerting his audience to the reality everyone knows: Jesus the Messiah of Israel has become Lord of all nations. One can say with Matthew that through Jesus Abraham has become the father of all peoples.

Conclusion

The introduction to Matthew's gospel concentrates on these factors: 1) Jesus is conceived through the Holy Spirit and so is divine; 2) he is Messiah of Israel and will be known as "God-with-us"; 3) his life will be threatened by Israelite authority and he will be worshipped by pagans; 4) he will be dedicated to God; even the name of his home town, Nazareth ("dedicated"), indicates this.

The story Matthew presents is one of growing tensions, tensions which help explain the death of Jesus with which his audience is familiar. Only at the end of the gospel do we hear the words of Jesus: "Go to all nations". Thus, the introduction is completed with the expected worship of pagans against the backdrop of rejection by many Jews.

Throughout the gospel there is an extended call to repentance and the life that follows upon repentance. Against this background there is the gradual unfolding of Jesus as Messiah. There are the Messianic qualities which were expected by the Jews: Jesus' power is immense, reminiscent in Jewish memory only of God himself. His holiness begins with his overcoming temptations and thereby showing his true mindset ("I will live from the word of God; I have no doubt of his love for me; I adore the Lord alone"). This mindset gradually reveals that the Messiah is to suffer for sins. And thus Jesus the Messiah, the Son of God, ends his life dying the crucifixion of a slave. The wisdom of Jesus is profound, and this wisdom is matched by his obedience to his Father to whom he has a special relation as Son. He is Messiah; more essentially, he is Son of God.

If one wonders about the meaning of Jesus as found in the account of his public life, one can only consult the many instances in which there is no explanation of him except to compare him with God. It is not for nothing that we read in Matthew the words filled with the deepest identity of Jesus: "No one knows the Son except the Father, and no one knows the Father except the Son" (11, 27). Through his actions and words he soars beyond Messiah to be "God-with-us".

Perhaps it was only fortuitous that Jesus came from Nazareth, but he certainly lived up to Matthew's understanding of this name as set forth in in the introduction to his gospel, for Jesus is the dedicated one. The introduction to Jesus' public life has served both to prepare the reader to follow the main lines of the gospel and to see in these main lines the fulfillment of the expectations which it arouses.

Luke

Luke's Introduction
Of the four gospels, Luke's is the only one which is not written to a community under oppression for its faith in Jesus, nor written by a Christian Jew. Luke is perhaps a Semite, but he is not a Jew. Luke writes in order that his reader "may comprehend how reliable are the things he has been taught". Luke's purpose, just cited, offers us two avenues for reflection. First, Luke seeks "comprehension'. Second, the reader is someone "who has already been taught things".

Comprehension
Luke's gospel is written to help a person comprehend: it is a matter then, first of all, of understanding. Certainly Luke wants to inspire his reader to an ever closer moral following of Jesus, for, as the Second Vatican Council states, every gospel is a preaching. But first of all Luke wants the reader to understand. The object of that knowledge, for which Luke assures his reader that he has done very careful research and study, is "reliability", or better, a greater reliability (or assuredness or certitude) about earlier teachings than the reader had enjoyed before taking up Luke's work. *One should leave Luke's work more convinced than ever about the things one had earlier and elsewhere been taught.*

The Traditions Known by Theophilus
Luke is concerned to show how reliable are "the things that had been taught". This sentence, together with his previous words, places Luke and his audience, represented by one member of the community, Theophilus, in the third generation of Christians. They depend on the handing on of traditions. So we ask what Theophilus has gained from the traditions, what these "teachings" are to which Luke refers. Can we identify them, so that we can better understand what Luke is concentrating on in his telling of the life of Jesus? On the one hand, we must admit that nowhere does Luke ever explicitly list or identify what his reader "has already been taught". On the other hand, we should consider four areas of thought that existed before Luke wrote and which probably go a long way to our identifying what teachings Luke is hoping to make appear ever more reliable.

Possible Pauline Influence

The letters of St. Paul are rightly famous. Their number, 13, represents almost one half of the total writings of the New Testament. This body of writing represents an enormous treasury of early Christian thought and served the young Church well in the second century when its doctrine needed defense and the New Testament canon was being defined. It is hard to imagine that Paul's theology as expressed in his letters, a theology which was so influential in the second Christian generation and all subsequent Christian thought, was not widely known throughout the Mediterranean world. While one can agree that certain Pauline teachings were unique to Paul and so not generally a part of Christian catechesis for new believers, many of his other theological principles certainly can be presumed to be known by anyone who became Christian. Luke may safely be presumed to be acquainted with Paul's thought since he seems to belong to a church founded by Paul and was a companion of Paul in the latter's last years.

Such theology included the meaning of the death and resurrection of Jesus, the teaching of a morality that represents traditions of the teaching of Jesus, emphases on helping the poor and on the virtues of charity and humility, particularly in forming and maintaining community, the beliefs in Father, Son and Holy Spirit, each of whom had a specific role in the salvation of the world. Indeed, the interpretation of the world according to Paul, based on the teachings of the Old Testament, were clearly taught to Jew and Gentile alike, especially the central notions of the call to be like God, the sin which brought death with it into the world, the salvation of human beings by the sacrificial and redeeming death of Jesus and the promise of life eternal. Added to these ideas are the reflections on the sacraments, particularly the Eucharist, on community and the ideal of love of neighbor. We recall, too, that much of what we find in the Pauline letters is not original with him, but material which upon his conversion he learned from tradition before him. We can never forget his stay of a year in the vibrant Christian community of Antioch-on-the-Orontes, where he learned to function as "prophet" and "teacher". Though we know few specifics about that stay, there seems little doubt that his views on Gentile and Jewish equality in God's church were developed here, and, again, he inherited much from those who theologized before him. All the letters of

Paul were completed twenty to twenty-five years before Luke wrote. Such a lively and powerful theology as Paul's must reflect a good deal of what was taught, in one form or another, to aspiring converts throughout the Mediterranean. As such they could hardly have failed to come to the avid attention of Luke. We should add that Luke, too, was a convert who knew from his own experience many of the teachings proposed to those who sought baptism, then learned more and more in their spiritual life.

Marcan Influence
A majority of scholars today are in agreement that Luke, like Matthew, used Mark's gospel as a source for his own work; he shares over 400 verses with Mark. This is reflected in Luke's use of many of Mark's stories, in the identical or nearly identical manner and placement in which we find them in Mark. Moreover, Luke has accepted as the outline of his own gospel the outline that Mark had used, stretching from baptism to resurrection, with one, final visit to Jerusalem. Finally, Luke has incorporated into his gospel principal theological themes of Mark. While one notes the differences between the two gospels, and finds it a fruitful and fascinating exercise to note how often Luke means to improve upon a Marcan story, the premise of such an exercise of course means that Luke is beginning with Mark in the first place. Mark was written about 70 AD, a fifteen years at least before Luke wrote. If one had a choice, it seems better to assume that Mark's interpretation of Jesus was well known in churches throughout the Mediterranean, and thus known to a person such as the convert Theophilus (the explicit object of Luke's Gospel [1, 1] and Acts [Acts of the Apostles 1, 1]).

Theophilus, according to Luke, is a believer; he must have had catechetical training, particularly in dealing with the confounding crucifixion of a person as "invincible" as Jesus. If we were to pick out a few of Mark's emphases, we surely should point to these: the power, wisdom and holiness of Jesus, which qualifies him to be called "Messiah"; the insistence of Jesus that Messiah can only be understood against the powerlessness, foolishness and servitude of his crucifixion; the need of the disciple to be ready to face the cross as Jesus did, whether to keep one's belief in Jesus or to remain faithful to the truths from the Father as he did; and an emphasis in the Christian life upon fidelity to God's will, love of neighbor and community, and humility .

Traditions Unique to Luke among the Gospels

When one thinks of the gospel of Luke, not far from our immediate recollection are the infancy stories in Luke's first two chapters. Where did Luke find these stories? Certainly Matthew, though agreeing with Luke on a number of points, has no record of them as Luke has them, nor can we ascribe them to Mark or other writings of the New Testament. Scholars call this Lucan material "Special Luke", to indicate that it is peculiar to his gospel. How many sources Luke drew upon for these stories we do not know, but clearly they are, in his mind, crucial for what he wants to achieve and are elements handed on to him and many others. Two examples of "Special Luke" are the famous parables of the prodigal son and of the good Samaritan, stories which underline, as do no others, the meaning of love of neighbor and of forgiveness. Luke inherited these stories; he was no eye-witness of Jesus. He did not make them up—and so we recognize, once again, how fruitful and rewarding was Luke's research of sources for his gospel and the likelihood that Theophilus had already been taught, if not all that Luke knew, at least something solid about the infancies of John and Jesus.

Summary

To end this portion of our reflection on the world prior to Luke, we can only conclude that, when one takes into account all the traditions that were current throughout the Christian Mediterranean, one has a sense of what must have been taught to Theophilus. As noted, we cannot define with certainty precisely what was taught to him and to others in his community, but recognizing Paul's popular work and the availability to Luke of many memorized and popular traditions in earliest Christianity, one can have a rather clear picture of the catechism which had been taught to Theophilus. It is this series of teachings that Luke means to strengthen when he says that he writes "that you, Theophilus, may comprehend how reliable are the things you have been taught". It is Luke's rendition of the life of Jesus and the subsequent movements of Christianity, through many countries, even to such a far away place as Rome, that will make this desired comprehension a reality for Theophilus and his fellow Christians. Luke and Theophilus are of the third generation, with Jesus and the missionaries who followed him in a second generation, but Luke has made sure of his sources, to the degree he could, and so becomes himself a sure source for the deeper understanding he wants for Theophilus and his community.

Luke's Introduction

Luke's gospel (and, we must also insist, Luke's Acts of the Apostles) is meant to show how reliable was teaching already received. We ask: how does Luke's introduction contribute to this goal? Since the introduction consists of seven narrated events (with the occasional summary story), we re-phrase our question: how does each of these seven events, now stories, help Luke convey the reliability of Christian catechesis to Theophilus and his community? What are Theophilus and his community to learn? These seven stories are: Gabriel's announcement to Zachary (1, 5-25); Gabriel's announcement to Mary [the annunciation] (1, 26-38); the meeting of Mary and Elizabeth, and Mary's song (1, 39-56); the naming of John together with Zachary's song (1, 57-80); the birth and circumcision/naming of Jesus (2, 2-21); the presentation of Jesus in the temple (2,22-40); the finding of Jesus in the temple (2, 41-51).

The first thought, given our goal, is that we should recognize that, whereas Luke's major source, Mark, has only one line of introduction, Luke has chosen seven stories. This can only mean, first, that Luke found Mark's introduction (though to be enfolded into the gospel of Luke) unsatisfactory for his purposes and, second, that all of these stories together serve as the fitting introduction to the adult Jesus as Luke wants to present him. One cannot ignore any one of them, if one is to understand all that Luke proposes for the understanding of Jesus, the hero of the public life to follow.

Now, though we do it after a manner which may remind one of lists in a telephone book, let us look at the Lucan teachings in these seven stories which help one understand clearly who the adult Jesus is and what God intends to accomplish through him.

Gabriel's Annunciation to Zachary

This first of seven stories or panels of the infancy narratives gives Theophilus the following certitudes. First, John will lead many of the children of Israel to the Lord their God. More specifically, he will come in the power and spirit of Elijah, the great prophet of the ninth century BC, the great prophet who called Israel to change in order to ready itself for the final judgment, who was so great that he never died and so was believed some day to return to earth to prepare a people fit for the Lord. Where Elijah's message bears fruit, he will be a source of great joy to Israel, whose faithful people had longed for the reestablishment of the covenant with God, for the arrival of the ever merciful and loving God. Second, Zachary's child will receive the name, John, a name which in Hebrew reveals that "God is gracious"; this name befits the message of forgiveness which John preaches to the repentant. Third, the remembrance of John's severe dress and food is explained as a sign of his role before God: to be a person dedicated totally to no other value than his mission. Finally, he will have the Holy Spirit of God from his conception. All of these elements should help Theophilus understand better the figure that preceded Jesus and the immense significance of John's pointing all believers beyond himself, to Jesus.

As is often the practice of Luke, however, there is not only revelation, but also response, and we see the poverty of Zachary's response in this first story. How can a human being say to an angel: "from whom can I find out if you are telling the truth?" Yet, that is what Zachary's bewilderment led him to ask. The proper response was trust, faith in the messenger of God, no matter how mysterious and impossible his words may seem; this is the virtue of the true Israelite and should be the virtue of Theophilus and his community.

Luke finishes this story with the first sign of God's new relationship with His people: Elizabeth, old like her husband Zachary and sterile and left to public embarrassment for not having a child to preserve the people of Israel, is saved from this shame; the proper response is joy. Here, before Jesus is born, is God's first act of mercy, as a part of the beginning of God's new plan to save Israel.

Gabriel's Annunciation to Mary

Luke's first choice was to begin his Gospel–Acts story with the definition of John the Baptist; now is the time he chooses to present to his audience a parallel but greater action which causes the very being of Jesus of Nazareth. This definition occurs in two moments. The first moment is the angel's revelation that Mary's child will be called "Jesus". (Matthew makes explicit what Luke intends implicitly: the name means "God causes salvation through the bearer of this name".) This savior will be understood to be the longed-for Messiah of Israel, the one who "will rule forever over the house of Jacob and his kingdom will have no end". If the sign of God's union with His beloved Israel is that God provide a noble, wise, holy, powerful ruler or king, the angel confirms that Jesus is this long-desired joy, the Messiah or king of Israel, often known as son of the great king David.

The second moment in Gabriel's revelation occurs in the definition of what it means to call Jesus "Son of God". Many people in Old Testament times were called son of God; for instance, a king, a prophet, a warrior, an angel and even Israel as one body of people were all called "son of God". Luke is very clear that this Son of God who is Jesus is totally different from others called son of God. Jesus' very being is divine, for he is son of God because the Power of the Most High and the Spirit of God created him in the womb of Mary. Thus, while others are sons of God by virtue of a gift to their being, Jesus is Son of God by his being, for he is unlike any-one else, conceived through the power of the Holy Spirit and the Power from on High. Luke uses a significant word here: "therefore" (1, 35). His sentence is: the Spirit will come upon you and the power from on high will overshadow you; *therefore* the child born of you will be called "Son of God". Luke here describes Jesus in terms of the immediate, superna-tural cause of his conception: if the immediate, supernatural cause of his conception is divine, then Jesus, the result of that cause, is divine.

Messiah and Son of God
Note that Luke has separated "Messiah" from "Son of God" in this an-nunciation from Gabriel. Luke's major source, Mark, began his gospel some fifteen years before Luke and wrote: the beginning of the good news of Jesus, Messiah and Son of God. Luke deliberately separates Mes-siah and Son of God: Son of God points to divinity as does no other title, including Messiah, and, to repeat, he makes it clear that Jesus is such be-cause his cause is divine. Thus, Luke can be said to want to present the ideas of Messiah and Son of God in two separate moments of the annun-ciation. He thereby makes clear the formal distinction between Messiah and Son of God. Luke will do the same in the trial of Jesus before the Sanhedrin. Mark combines the titles in this trial, but Luke separates them and speaks of each of them as distinct, the one from the other.

We should here note again that we are in the midst of Luke's two chapter introduction to Luke–Acts, and that this means that what is said here is to be carried through every moment of the entire subsequent story to which this is introduction. Though we rarely see the title "Son of God" used in Luke–Acts, we should keep it in mind as we read through this entire work, for this is to respect the very nature of the introduction.

Mary's Response to the Announcement

Gabriel's announcement to Mary about the meaning of Jesus is not the only value of Luke's famous annunciation story. To the revelations from Gabriel must be added the profound response of Mary. It is almost as if a story which began as revelation ends in a story characterized as mission, for indeed Mary's assent, "Behold the handmaid of the Lord", is her willing acceptance of the role she is now asked to play. Her obedience is open-ended: she says "yes" to many years of raising a child with love. This fourteen-ear-old girl "signs up" for the future that she cannot foresee: the wonder of her child who grows into such a teacher acting with such power, a child who will face such bitter acrimony and antipathy leading even to crucifixion, and a child who will then rise to glory. How could she ever know all this? And yet, at this moment before Gabriel, she says "yes" to it all, for she is and ever will be the handmaid of the Lord: she will always accept His will. As in the case of Zachary, so here too, Luke writes not only of God's revelation to human beings, but of human beings' response to God. It takes more reading of Luke to understand what we say now at the start: Mary is not only an individual remembered with affection 85 or 90 years after conceiving Jesus, but she is, in Luke's eyes, a model for the Christian, and for the Church, for she loves and obeys in all circumstances, even if she does not fully understand.

The Relationship between Jesus and John

A point to note regards the relationship between Jesus and John. John's public life as preacher and baptizer began before Jesus' public life. John preached repentance and a return to obedience to the Mosaic Law; John's baptism was an action by which one publicly announced one's repentance prayed for moral purity and new life. John does not forgive sins, but the actions of John and the repentant presume that God will. When Jesus came onto the scene, after he was baptized by John, Jesus preached repentance as a requisite for entering the Kingdom of God. How was he different from John? Indeed, John was highly revered by many in Israel, and we read of his disciples as still existing in 50 AD, well after he died. What was his relationship to the younger Jesus? Christians developed an understanding that we see expressed in Luke's introduction. John is preparing people for the final judgment, but, in accord with Luke's text at 3, 15-18, he is also preparing the way of the Lord Jesus. His baptism is only a prefiguring of the baptism Jesus will give, for Jesus will give in baptism what John cannot give: the Holy Spirit of God who is the source of all morality and God-likeness. Jesus will be divine and the king within the kingdom of God; anyone whose life is based on his words, not those of Moses, will enjoy the kingdom of heaven. Jesus is the longed-for fulfillment of Israel's deepest hopes. For centuries Israel has waited for him, and now he is here. Jesus himself forgives sins.

Luke eventually provided a clear picture of how two great preachers, contemporaries, relate to each other, but the picture has already, in its essentials, been drawn in the introduction. As all gospels remind their readers: "there is one coming greater than I; I am not worthy to be his servant". John had an earthly father; Jesus had did not. John had the Holy Spirit once he was conceived; Jesus' very conception was caused by the Holy Spirit of God. One should also add that, according to the four gospels, Jesus worked miracles whereas John did not. Further, Jesus expiated the sins of the world, John did not. And John did not rise from the grave to sit at the right hand of the Father as judge of the world. No doubt, inasmuch as they both initially were involved with baptism with water (cf. John 3, 22; 4, 1-2), it was difficult for many at the time of the beginning of Jesus' public ministry to separate the two; it is the rest of their lives, and reflection on them, that makes their relationship clear.

Why John never became a public disciple of Jesus is explained in no gospel, nor in any other writing. This, as suggested above, adds to the confusion about the meaning of the two preachers. Perhaps the best we can say is that the uniqueness of Jesus, as experienced in his public life, became clearer and clearer only after the martyrdom of John.

Mary's Visit to Elizabeth

When Mary arrives to help Elizabeth through her last months of childbearing, Elizabeth is for the moment inspired to be a prophetess. In her womb leaps her child, an event which becomes a sign of a secret wisdom working within her. As a result of this sign from her son, Elizabeth knows that Mary is carrying Elizabeth's Lord, and she publicly calls him such. It is the first time Jesus is called "Lord" in Luke, a title usually reserved for the divinity; its recognition is owed to prophetic insightfulness. Elizabeth speaks with the knowledge of God.

Mary's response to Elizabeth is, as Luke sees it, a further reflection by Mary on her situation. She had been struck in wonder at being called "full of grace", and asked "how" she could conceive without male cooperation, and professed obedience at the word of her Lord. Now she is presented with a further reflection on what has happened to her. In response to this prophecy from Elizabeth Mary sings a hymn, for centuries called the Magnificat because in the Latin version of her words "Magnificat" (= "makes glorious", i.e., thus Mary declares God glorious) is the first word of her song. Mary's famous song or poem has three parts.

Mary Blessed and Made Glorious
First, verses 46-49 tell of the glory Mary receives as mother of Jesus, who is conceived in her through the power of God. Mary had seen herself as one of the countless millions who live, die and are eventually forgotten. Not so, she reflects, now that she is the mother of the divine Jesus, she will be remembered for all ages, thanks to God's choice of her as Jesus' mother.

God's Help to Israel in All Ages
Second, with verses 50-54 Mary begins to see that His mercy, which has visited her, is upon all who fear Him, that what has happened to her is simply the latest expression of God's immense love for the lowly and the poor. Indeed, she says, His mercy is from age to age; she knows this in particular from God's munificence to Israel, who, when so many times poor and lowly, was saved by God. Now Mary realizes that what God has done for her is part of the continual plan of God to form Israel, and then the world, as Genesis says, "…in the image and likeness of God".

Mary and Jesus, the Latest of God's Graces to Israel
Third, in verse 55 Mary shows that she now understands that what had been done for her and in her, and what God had done over the centuries

for many Israelites who needed God's help against tyranny and pride and wealth, all that is rooted in the initial promise of God to Abraham, that He would most unexpectedly provide children to Abraham and his offspring, more than the stars in the heavens and the sands on the seashore. God's people will be great and glorious, no matter what the opposition. If at first she speaks to Elizabeth of God's blessing, she quickly sees that what has been given to her is just the latest of God's acts of kindness to Israel, and in fact it is rooted in the founding blessing to "Abraham and to his offspring".

One senses that the author has introduced his story in such a way as to place Jesus within a plan of God which begins with God's revelation about John before he is conceived and will play itself out through all of the gospel and Acts: with the final words of the Magnificat we realize that since Abraham there has been a plan of God for salvation, a plan now giving us Jesus. There is a greatness here which is rooted in God himself. On this score, Luke's gospel is not only a book about Jesus; it is a book, together with Acts, about God's plan of salvation for all nations. Luke distinguishes himself from other evangelists precisely by requiring his reader to follow his story from the announcement to Zachary to Paul in Rome.

From this point of view Mary's song is one of the Lucan elements that indicate that our interest is not supposed to be limited to the public life of Jesus, important as that is. It is better to speak of a divine plan depending on the initiative of God and described by Luke throughout the gospel and Acts. This plan which Luke details extends all the way to Paul in house arrest in Rome in 61-63 AD. The annunciation of Gabriel to Zachary, not the annunciation of Gabriel to Mary, is Luke's initial intervention of God in His decision concerning the account of Jesus' part in that plan. What is of interest to Luke, then, is not simply the public life of Jesus, but the divine plan in which the public life of Jesus plays a major and central, but limited, part. One need only think of Pentecost and of the decisions about Cornelius and other Gentiles (Chapters 10–11, 18 and Chapter 15) to realize that there was more to God's entry into the world than the public life of Jesus. God's anger, as Paul says, is abated and replaced by His desire to declare all people just and sinless again in covenant with Himself. And that change is manifested not solely in the coming of Jesus, but in the coming of John the Baptist, and continues beyond the first and second generations of the first century AD until today and beyond. It is this insight which moved Luke to write two volumes, gospel and Acts. Luke saw the hand of God in all that transpired from the announcement of the birth of John the Baptist through Paul's years in Rome. It is only with this entire story that Luke can hope to provide for Theophilus a true comprehension of the things he had been taught.

Zachary, His Child and His Song
This final story of Chapter 1 begins with Zachary's insistence, now in obedience to the revelation of Gabriel, that his son be named John. Is there any question, once Zachary begins to speak after nine months of enforced silence, about the divine definition of John ["God-is-gracious"]? By reading these stories as stories of divine revelation, Theophilus begins to be ever more sure about the things he has been taught.

Zachary's Reflection on Jesus and John
Mary had offered her reflection about the meaning of what had happened to her. Now it is Zachary's turn to sing about what God has done in both Jesus and John. In the song, Zachary, now prophet because inspired by the Holy Spirit, speaks directly only to his son, John, and surrounds the image of John with more forceful images of the mighty Jesus. In this way the very structure of the song shows at the same time the place of John within the Jesus reality and John's inferiority to Jesus. Zachary's hymn offers two reflections about Jesus. First, he is to be understood as a mighty savior who frees us from even our most powerful enemies. Second, he is to be understood as the light by which we can follow the path to the deepest and most lasting, most valuable peace, that with God.

Jesus as Mighty Savior
Often the idea of salvation is a confined to our exiting this life and entering eternal life; in this framework, salvation occurs at the end of one's life. In Zachary's song things are different. Here he emphasizes a savior who saves us *now* so that we might fulfill the highest dignity of a human being: to worship God in holiness and justice all the days of our lives. Who can free us so that we may act properly as creatures towards the Creator? Jesus the savior will do that *now*, so that, once freed, the rest of our lives will be lived in holiness and justice. In Jesus God provides the di-

vine power to save. Praise to God, Zachary says, for Jesus!

Jesus as Light

Many people over the ages have defined human beings, and they often come up short in their definitions. Zachary has a definition of human existence: we live in darkness and in the shadow of death. No matter how good our present health and how pleasant the world around us, we are in reality in darkness and so near to death that we can be said to be daily in its presence. Who can free me from darkness and death so that I may find peace? Who can light up the darkness for me? Who can lead me beyond the darkness of death? This definition of Jesus shows that God, while providing us with divine power, also provides us with the only illumination which will light our way to peace with Him. Power (verses 68-75) and Light (verses 78-79) are two strong images, each of which in its own way further defines Jesus.

Finally, between references to Jesus, in his song Zachary refers to his son, John (verses 76-77). He does this because, in his own way, John can be said to participate in salvation. Not only is he to prepare the way of the Lord Jesus, the Savior; he is also, through his baptizing, to help people to experience salvation. For what is forgiveness of a repentant sinner if not a saving act of God? John does not forgive, as does Jesus, but his preaching and baptism express the hope, based on confidence in God's unending love, that all will be forgiven. Such is the symbolism of the washing with water: being cleaned, indeed rising from death to life.

The Contributions of the Magnificat and the Benedictus

It is good to make explicit that the songs of Mary and Zachary further the initial revelations given to Zachary and Mary. What Zachary and Mary sang can be found in Gabriel's announcements of to them only with difficulty. But when Gabriel's words have been illumined by their songs the plan of the saving God becomes ever clearer. Especially as all that is said is the result of prophecy which is God's word spoken through human beings. Luke believes he will assure Theophilus, as never before, of the solidity of what Theophilus had been taught, for it is patently God who is behind all salvation.

Jesus' Birth

After the revelations of Gabriel and reflections upon them, Luke advances his story to the birth of Jesus and events surrounding it. There are a number of things in this story that Luke thinks will help Theophilus better appreciate the things he has been taught. To understand the first point, it is good to recall that Theophilus is not Jewish, but Gentile, and not a person of Jesus' generation, but two or three generations later; like Luke himself, Theophilus has scant detailed knowledge of Israel, the scene of Jesus' public life. Indeed, on a number of counts Theophilus is quite a different person than those Jews who followed Jesus in Galilee to his death in Jerusalem or those who made up earliest Christianity. To put it briefly, Luke has to update the story of Jesus to fit a new generation and new Mediterranean geography, and make sense to a mindset that knows nothing about Judaism and the Old Testament, which were the foundation of Jesus' own life and preaching. Indeed, how should one make fully intelligible events which, of themselves, are quite foreign to Theophilus' historical past and sociological present, to his ways of thinking and acting?

With a view to his non-Jewish but Rome-dominated audience, Luke first fits the birth of Jesus into a list of the major rulers of the then-known world, the world with which Theophilus is more familiar. Theophilus did not live under the old rulers Luke now and in Chapter 3, 1-2 identifies, but Roman rule with its phalanx of officials was a reality of public life well known and appreciated by Theophilus. The Jesus-event, then, is to be fixed against a "universal" history, that of the Roman Empire with its tentacles even in Syria and Palestine. This birth is no longer just a tiny event in a poorly known piece of territory at the eastern end of the Mediterranean Sea, but an event of world history. As Luke presents him, Jesus the savior, born in Bethlehem, is a citizen in the broad sense not just of Israel, but of the entire Roman Empire.

Every adult male was ordered by Quirinius, Luke tells us, to go to his hometown to register. This was a plan by which the Romans knew how to apportion taxes. Certainly, the arrival of so many outsiders made it impossible for some to find lodging. Joseph had a particular problem, because, having decided that he could not leave his wife at this moment of birth, brought her with him and had to provide some housing for her in this critical moment. Caves dotted the hillsides around Bethlehem. They were places where shepherds would keep their sheep by night in the inner recesses with food for them in a manger, while they slept in the forward part, protecting the flock. While it is understandable how Mary and Joseph came to pass the night in a cave in which the child was born and then placed in a manger, one cannot but marvel at the poverty of the situation. These circumstances show the kind of savior now being born, the love that thus enters into the world in sympathy for all and not just for some, the love that wants to share our lives. And a love which was not concerned for the person of Jesus.

One can debate about the poverty level of shepherds in Jesus' time, but it is clear that few people today in the West want to live under conditions that characterized shepherding 2000 years ago in Palestine. But it is also clear that, as with us in our day, there was wealth in Israel far beyond anything a shepherd or we would imagine. The shepherds, even against the standards of their own time (not to mention ours), were poor, but in addition they were "unclean", as the Mosaic Law calls those who engage in such an occupation, unworthy to stand and pray with men before God. For the sheep is defined as an inherently unclean animal—if one touches it one cannot come before God in public prayer until one is cleaned by a temple sacrifice. It was to these "little ones" (not necessarily "holy ones") that the angelic message is given.

The angel's message counts on Theophilus' knowing the essentials of Jewish faith, specifically the concept of the covenant, i.e., the agreement between two parties. Covenant was a very useful human experience by which to describe the intimate relationship between God and His creature. In this concept, two partners agree to union, and each offers the other all it possibly can. It is like marriage (which itself is often called a covenant and in some ways surpasses "covenant"). When the angel announces that peace and good will now come to earth, he means to say that God now plans to create another, new covenant with Israel. For God, the past is now forgiven and forgotten. He shows this to mankind by His Son's own living a human life "like us, in all things save sin" (Hebrews 4, 14) and dying for us. Indeed, this partner is giving all He has, the Father giving the Son, for us.

The angel announces a great joy, and this birth should bring great gladness, for here is born the Savior who is Christ and Lord. While one can, for simplicity's sake, treat these three titles as one, it is better to recognize

that each title has its own meaning and thus adds its own contribution to
the rich meaning of Jesus. Christ as Messiah and Lord is a person who is
to provide the greatest benefits to all people living in his kingdom; no one
is excluded from these maximum blessings. Rare indeed is the Messiah
who has the power, wisdom and holiness to benefit all in his kingdom—
but Jesus does. "Lord" suggests two ideas. First, a lord is one who com-
mands, and all obey. Second, a lord is one who has power. Jesus is introduced to the shepherds as lord, for all he need do (and his public life
continually shows this) is command, and obedience, whether of man or of
nature or of demons, is total and immediate. And who can question the
power of Jesus? He who dominates nature, sin, death, all physical and
psychological ills, and the demon world, over which no human being has
control? But neither of these titles means, of itself, "Savior". For savior
implies the need to be "saved from that from which I cannot save myself". Savior implies power and wisdom, but more, it implies the essential
good will to save me who, left to myself, am powerless and lost. Salvation has as much to say about the human being's condition as it does
about God's desire to save. Such is the pattern of human concepts which
will help Theophilus soon appreciate better who this Jesus is in whose
name he has been baptized.

Joy, praise and peace are the logical conclusions to having in one's
midst a covenant partner who will provide all the promised benefits one
can imagine, one who dominates all for the benefit of his people, and one
who saves from all from which I cannot save myself. In it not difficult to
understand that a people accustomed to these titles and longing for generations for the coming of this person should joyfully tell everyone in sight
that he is born.

It will be very useful to recall later, when reading the public life of Jesus and the tension over the question of his being the Messiah, that Jesus
was born in Bethlehem. Everyone knew the tradition that the eventual
great Messiah of Israel would come from David's family, a family that
had its roots in no other place than Bethlehem. Geography itself, then,
argues that Jesus is the Messiah, *the* awaited descendant from David. In
the gospel of John the author records the question which shows the importance of Bethlehem in the definition of Messiah, "Surely, does not the
scripture say that the Messiah, being of David's family, is to come from
Bethlehem [Micah 5, 1], the village where David lived?" (John 7, 42).

How is Mary pictured amidst the joy spread by the exuberant shepherds? While many rejoiced and praised God for His divine entry into our world and for his new covenant, in Mary's case Luke introduces pondering and meditation: Mary "reflects upon all these things in her heart". For Luke understands that, while many rejoiced at what they understood but only in a limited way, there was need to think long and hard about this child and God Himself.

As at the annunciation and visitation, Mary now shows herself not just to be an individual, but also to be the ideal disciple. As an individual, she ponders the meaning given to her about her son. Yes, she had heard him described as Messiah, holy and Son of God (1, 31-33.35), but she had not known him under the title of savior, and that title opens up a field of thought that runs through the life of the Church, as Jesus comes not only to rule and to bless, but also to save. She must ponder that. As a model disciple, Mary, standing for each of us, tries to understand her God ever more deeply. In this, Luke hopes that Theophilus will have the mind of Mary, to think out the will of God as thoroughly as she, all the time faithful in embracing it.

It is interesting to note that though Mary had been told much about her child at the annunciation, she still needs to meditate in order to understand the full implications of her son. Putting it differently, she was not able to say to the shepherds that, in light of the annunciation, she already knew all this that was new to them. No, rather she learned from experience to experience who Jesus was, and always awaited in trust and obedience for the next revelation about him and about her own future.

Jesus Forty Days after His Birth
According to Moses, a woman was obliged to purify herself forty days after her first male child was born and to offer to God an offering which was in place of what should be the true offering, her son. The purification of the woman was essential, so that she could take her place in the temple for proper worship of God. What was impure about her was her spilling blood and other internal liquids at the birth moment. While many centuries before Mary's time the rule about purification was made because those birth liquids were considered unhealthy for anyone to touch (and so the woman had to be certified as healthy to be able to return to the community), in Mary's time this rule had become predominantly a religious

requirement. All things defined in the Mosaic Law as impure or defined as causing impurity in others needed purification so that a person could worship God in proper dignity and be no harm to those about him. It was Jesus' insight into the matter of purification which introduced the true legislation: it is in moral matters, not physical situations, that a person must stay away from the community (that is, being excommunicated) until purified. In this, Jesus "brought the Mosaic Law to perfection", as Matthew says (5, 17).

The basis of Jesus' parable about the good Samaritan is another and famous example of the rule about touching impure things, in this case the impurity of a dead body. We recall that, in that imaginary moment, the priest and the Levite would have nothing to do with the presumed dead body of an Israelite. That was because the Mosaic Law indicated that one should stay way from dead bodies, not touch them, or one will be unable to worship God worthily in public until one is ritually cleansed. For this reason the priest and Levite did not help the fallen Israelite. A Samaritan, looked upon in Jewish storytelling to be impure, felt no obligation to keep the Mosaic Law in this situation, and so he tends to the wounded Israelite and becomes the object of Jesus' praise.

Two Major Points in This Sixth Panel

There are two major points that Luke wants Theophilus to take from this sixth panel of the introduction. They have to with the revelation that the old man Simeon gave to Mary and Joseph regarding Jesus. It is the first time that Luke explicitly 1) suggests an opening of Jesus to the Gentiles and 2) reveals Jesus' life to be a life of contestation, for the benefit of or not of others.

Simeon is a figure symbolizing the Old Testament as embodies the relationship of God to Israel as it was known up to his time. This man who symbolizes the "old" recognizes that what he had longed for was now at hand, in his arms, at his breast. He symbolically notes that he, who represents the time of hoping, can pass on, now that the new divine intervention has actually taken root in Israel. Hope ceases with possession of what was hoped for.

The Gentile and the Acts of the Apostles

Once again Luke thinks that the idea "salvation" is an excellent way to describe the meaning of Jesus. But now Jesus, already identified as the salvation of Israel, is to be the salvation prepared for all nations. Here, as is characteristic of an introduction of a book, a new idea comes alive and will reach from the beginning of Jesus' public life to the end of Luke's second volume, the Acts of the Apostles. For the first time, Luke explicitly indicates that his story will reach further than Israel, indeed "to the end of the earth" (Acts 1, 8). We will see just how Jesus will save all nations, Israel first then the Gentiles, but Luke gives us two descriptions which help anticipate what we will read.

First, Jesus will be the light for the nations. Zachary had sung about Jesus that he would be the light from on high to enlighten our way to peace with God (1, 79). At this juncture, Luke intended to describe the enlightenment of Israel. But many of Luke's statements are applicable to the entire world, once one learns that God's plan to save is universal in scope. Again, given that Acts will follow the triumphant march of the saving plan of God through the pagan world, Luke emphasizes this significant description of "light", for "life in darkness", i.e., without the true God and His wisdom. This is the Jewish description of Gentiles. For Luke, the wisdom, the teaching of Jesus stood out as one of his most powerful and inspiring characteristics. "All the people hung on his every word" (Luke 19, 48) is a picture which describes Jesus' contemporaries and Luke himself and, he knows, the community to whom he writes. It is because of Jesus' wonderful teaching that Luke has expanded the gospel of Mark to include so many (11) new parables (particularly we note the parable of the good Samaritan and the parable of the prodigal son) and to present a defining sermon at the mount (Luke 6). Finally, it is through his disciples, his witnesses "to the end of the earth" (Acts 1, 8), that Jesus will save all nations.

The Glory of Israel
Second, Jesus will be the glory of Israel. When one hears "glory" one instinctively looks for the reason, and in scriptures the reason for glory is God. Israel, in the New Testament times as well as in many earlier centuries, was humbled by foreign conquest and the subsequent loss of religious freedom that involved. Human thought embraced the idea that God would intervene to free Israel from its submission to Rome and be its own

free state. For Luke the freedom brought by Jesus to Israel was not political; it was a release from many other evils, not the least of which was sin. Now, to win these many freedoms there must be power to win. Israel did not have this, whether to free itself from Rome or from the many other evils that beset it (sicknesses, demon possessions, death itself). Being so handicapped, Israel had no basis for glory. It possessed no person or reason to merit glory. It was helpless. Simeon now says that Israel will be glorified, but indicates clearly that the reason, the basis for Israel's glory will be solely Jesus. He is the one because of whom Israel will be glorified. There will be many moments in the public life of Jesus which are saving moments for Israelites. And then there will be that moment in which Jesus will pour out his blood for the forgiveness of sins. Israel could not free itself from the evils which beset it; Jesus will free Israel and so be the reason or grounds for Israel's being called "glorious".

Jesus, for the Rise and Fall of Many
If Simeon was the first to suggest explicitly that Jesus is the salvation of all nations, he is also the first to introduce the reality that Jesus would be "for the rise and the fall of many in Israel". It will take the reading of the gospel and Acts to see more clearly, precisely what "rise" and "fall" imply. But already in a general way from his experience Theophilus would read into these words the beginnings and growth of the Christian Church, on the one hand, and the denial and ultimate rejection of Jesus by many in Israel and elsewhere. Indeed, at the moment it is obscure, yet predictable by those who already know the story: Jesus will even be put to death by many of those who refuse him. Jesus will force the issue of choice: whatever one may think privately and secretly about him, eventually a choice must be made, either for him or against him: all hearts must be revealed in his regard, some even to the nefarious act of crucifixion.

Mary is again portrayed to Theophilus, now as one who will suffer at her son's suffering. As she is present through most of the introduction, Luke uses her now as an individual intimately involved her son's life, and as a symbol of the life of every believer that is entwined in the life of Jesus.

Anna and "Liberation"
Luke completes this sixth panel of his introduction with the figure of An-

na, a prophetess (that is, one who speaks on behalf of God and through whom God speaks). She, like Simeon, is described as "old", so one is to see in her, as in Simeon, a figure completing the Old Testament era. She speaks of redemption, a redemption that clearly has Jesus at its center. A dictionary would define "redemption" as a "buying back for a price". However the Old Testament often ignores that dictionary definition (God pays no one a price to have His people back) and prefers to speak of redemption as "liberation" or "setting free" from some kind of servitude. The most important use of the term "redemption" in this way is the Exodus, which the Old Testament describes as a freedom or redemption from slavery in Egypt. As the Exodus experience of Israel became the fundamental experience by which Israel described the Lord's freeing Israel, so now Jesus is described as the fundamental experience by which God frees "all the nations".

Luke's Summary

As with many introductions to biography in the first century AD (and to some degree Luke's gospel is biographical), Luke leaves strict storytelling to refer with a few verses and in general terms to the growth of the child Jesus, from this moment of forty days old to the age of twelve. As most "heroes" have a childhood that will not contradict, but rather promote and anticipate the greatness of the hero as an adult, Luke so presents Jesus. What is perhaps worth a moment's recognition is the fact that Jesus, though described as divine, grew in a normal way; particularly stressed, in another summary at the end of the introduction, is the obedience of Jesus to his parents, the most visible example of his proper growth in "grace". Granted that Jesus will show at twelve years old a precociousness which startles adults (for Luke does not present a Jesus as an adult in a child's body), but he is also a child who has learned his Old Testament lessons well and now, in a moment which anticipates his adult wisdom, puts them on display.

Jesus in the Temple

Luke concludes his introduction with a story taken from a time when Jesus was twelve years old. The story signals the piety of this young person who, at the age of twelve (Jewish tradition formally obliged a young man beginning at the age of 13) and in still under the care of his parents, begins to assume the responsibilities of obeying the Mosaic Law. Here Jesus expresses his assumption of these duties by going to worship God in Jerusalem at Passover time. This responsibility of obedience to God will be called "accepting the burden", a phrase Jesus will use later when he says that his yoke (unlike that of the authoritative teachers of Israel) is easy, his burden light.

Customs to Consider
How did it come to be that Jesus was lost? Our story assumes the possibility that not before the completion of a day's journey away from Jerusalem would a parent know that his child is missing. This has to do with the custom of traveling in groups. It was advisable, for safety reasons, to travel from Nazareth to Jerusalem in large groups, family joining other families for the trip, and this leads to dividing the groups into three: men together, women together and children together. Our story assumes this way of traveling for the holy family. The journey, on foot and about eighty-five miles from Nazareth to Jerusalem, took at minimum five days. For safety's sake, most of the journey took place on the east bank of the Jordan River, thereby avoiding hostile Samaria.

The worship at Passover is not the issue in this remembrance of the boy Jesus and his parents. The story picks up after the celebration of the feast, with the journey back to Nazareth. It happened that Mary and Joseph, after being separated for a day, met together, to be joined, they thought, by their child to spend the night together. But the child did not appear.

Circumstances of the Story
Concerned, Mary and Joseph returned to Jerusalem where they had last seen Jesus. And they searched the city for a long while, till on the third day they finally found him in the temple. We recall that Jerusalem at this time, though the capital of Judah, was certainly no larger than two miles by two miles. Moreover, by the word "temple" Luke indicates the platform (a bit larger than a football or soccer field) on which the central building of worship, the temple, was built. Jesus' being found occurs not in this particular building, but in another area on this large platform and adjacent to the most holy site of worship. We remember that it was in the

actual temple building and not simply on the temple platform, that Zachary received the revelation that he would have a son, John. In our case now, we are not in that temple building, but somewhere close to it. Now begins the drama, the resolution of which is the point Luke wants to emphasize to Theophilus as Luke gives his seventh story and finally exits from his two chapters of introduction.

The precise point at issue here is where Jesus is in Jerusalem. Mary's anxious question begins with the observation that she and Joseph had been searching for Jesus for three days. This can only mean that they did not know where to look for him, that in their judgment he could be anywhere. The answer of Jesus appears rather unfeeling, given the worried state of his parents. He does nothing more than insist that they should have known where to find him: they should have looked immediately to the temple, the house of his Father, for surely they know him to be his Father's Son?

We can divide Luke's teachings from this story of the finding of the child Jesus in the temple into two parts: obedience and wisdom. The first part has three points to it.

Obedience

We cannot emphasize too much that Luke has decided that this, and no other, be his final introductory story. This is the conclusion of all he wanted to say in his introduction. It must be important. It is with Luke's teaching of this story that we go forward to the adult life of Jesus, even while remembering all that we have already been taught about Jesus in this introduction. And what is this teaching here, this emphasis? It is that Jesus, whatever other title may be given him, is especially to be remembered as Son of God. It is under that title that we are particularly to read the adult life of Jesus. We recall that Son of God was the title the angel Gabriel revealed to Mary at her annunciation. No matter what else was said of Jesus in the introduction (e.g., Messiah, savior, Lord, light of Israel and of the nations, glory of Israel, redeemer), it is the title "Son of God" which Luke puts at the end of his introduction, asking us to interpret Jesus with the meaning of that title.

However, "Son of God" has two meanings, both of which Luke applies now to Jesus. One is the sense in which a person is identified as divine in being. Another is the sense in which a person is identified as Son of God because he is obedient, like a son to his father—in this case, the obedience of the divine Son to his Father. Without forgetting the revelation of Gabriel, that "they will call him Son of God" because his conception is caused by a divine action, it is this latter sense that Luke emphasizes as Jesus says to his parents, "Is it not necessary that I be in my Father's house, doing my Father's work?"

When Luke subsequently narrates the baptism (3, 21-22) and the temptations of Jesus (4, 1-13), the term Son of God will be used, explicitly or implicitly. In those uses, it is the obedience of Jesus which is emphasized. Indeed, it will be Jesus' perfect obedience to his Father that characterizes his entire public life, his agony in the garden, and explains his subsequent attitude throughout his suffering and death. While Luke puts great emphasis on Jesus' obedience as a son, he intends to say, from the story of the annunciation, that the obedience we see throughout the gospel is that of a divine person become human towards his divine Father.

Luke follows through on his presentation of Mary in this gospel introduction. Again, she shows that she does not realize the full implication of her son's being Son of God. Because she learned from Gabriel that Jesus will be conceived not through human, but through divine action, it does not follow that she knew and anticipated every step that divine Sonship would take. Despite what she learned before an event, she must continue to learn through (often suffering through) a new event or saying. In this, she is very much the image of every Christian we will meet in Luke's work and of Theophilus himself. Indeed, though now far away, Luke will describe Mary in the Acts of the Apostles as one waiting with other faithful followers of Jesus for the gift of the Holy Spirit. Her guidance by God seems to come in stages, and this, Luke understands, makes her more than ever a model and inspiration for all Jesus' followers. In his introduction, Luke's last description of her is in his expression, "His mother kept all these things in her heart" (2, 51). With Mary, one is always led back to her fundamental saying: "If this is what You want, I will do it; I do not understand, but I trust You and will obey" (1, 38).

There is no mistaking the note of independence here. That is, Jesus is made to appear quite independent of his parents. His response to his anxious and worried parents could seem cold and even cheeky. But Luke's presentation of Jesus wants to emphasize, even at the cost of apparent insensitivity, Jesus' radical determination to obey only his Father. Even now the lesson is taught that Jesus follows the will of his Father, that his physical relationships take second place to his relationship with his Father. In showing this sense of independence, Luke prepares the reader for the obvious independence we will see in Jesus the adult. This is not to say that we can conclude that Jesus was not attached to his parents in the fullest sense, emotionally and intellectually; it only says that, for all his union with them, he has an attachment which is more profound than any other enjoyed by human beings. On the contrary, one can say that it is Jesus' psychological make-up that makes him an exquisitely sensitive being, even in regard to sinners. God is his center, as our final story shows, and this center is Himself love of everyone. Such is the psychological make-up of Jesus, shown even now at twelve years old, the moment Luke chooses first to speak about it.

But the question of Jesus' obedience is more demanding than what we have described thus far. It is Luke who, now responsible for a summary as the holy family proceeds home from Jerusalem, singles out the fact that Jesus "went down with them (from the mountain on which Jerusalem is situated)...and was obedient to them" (2, 51). Independent so as to be obedient to his Father, yes, but then also obedient to his parents. For a moment he was separate from them, but now he is shown to be "with them".

Wisdom

Embedded in this story is the wisdom of Jesus, a foreshadowing of that public life in which Jesus manifests his profound knowledge of God and of life. During the period of searching for him, Jesus is near the temple building, in the midst of the teachers of Israel, in their accustomed place of teaching on the temple platform, where he listens to them and asks them questions (2, 46-47). The reaction is noteworthy, indeed defining: all who listened to him were astonished at his understanding and his answers. Now, the boy is only twelve years old, and here Luke wants him understood as such. But within this age limitation Jesus already appears to astound the best teachers, with questions and with his own answers. The question raised elsewhere about John the Baptist is pertinent here: "What will this child be?" (1, 66).

The wisdom Jesus represents is a central aspect of his adult life. Jesus was not crucified because reports about his childhood, or because of his miracles (who would want those to stop?). If Jesus deserved to be "put away" he deserved it because of his teaching, or, better, because of the challenge his teaching presented to the dominant teaching or wisdom of authoritative specialists in the interpretation of the Law of the time. The Law of Moses was crucial, Israel understood, for the well-being of the people of Israel. He who followed false wisdom was sure to anger God and bring severe punishment. No one must ever change the Law of Moses! True, many scribes and Pharisees and various groups of priests became envious of Jesus and he was a threat to their rule over the people. But their essential argument against Jesus was his claim that he knew better than anyone else what the will of God was. Given this tension in Jesus' adult life, we see how Luke has prepared us already with the twelve-year-old Jesus for what was to come in the rest of his story.

Conclusion

Clearly Luke has gone to great lengths to introduce his reader to the adult Jesus. Unlike his source Mark, Luke offers a plethora of figures, most of whom reflect the Old Testament writings and thought. Each of these figures offers a particular glimpse of the person of Jesus; no one figure says it all. Perhaps because Luke is attempting to have his reader comprehend the reliability of many elements of the reader's Christian education, Luke brings into his introduction titles of Jesus that other evangelists, for their particular purposes, might not use. For the gospels of Mark, Matthew and John are aimed above all at helping Christians who suffer under extreme criticism, if not actual persecution and death, for what they believe. Luke's audience, explicitly represented by Theophilus, has other concerns than threats to faith.

As for a conclusion, it is best simply to re-read the seven stories Luke has told, while asking oneself what in this story could make Christian teaching more reliable and, as well, how this "reliability" is achieved. Meanwhile, we now highlight two of Luke's major insights or teachings. We divide the introduction into two parts.

First, Luke wrote his two volumes, gospel and Acts, because the gospel alone is not sufficient for his purposes. The unity of the two volumes is one of the most visible reasons why Luke did not want simply to copy and send off to Theophilus the gospel of Mark. Mark had his own interests in writing a gospel: answers to Christians under oppression in Rome. Luke had no problem like oppression and hatred to contend with; rather, he wanted to lead Theophilus into "thinking big", to be ever more deeply aware of the reality that God had a plan of salvation that began in Israel, but was destined to reach to the ends of the earth. Theophilus should know this plan in order to understand how it was that Christianity reached *him*, defined *him*, and gave *him* the true God to worship and obey. Indeed, intriguing and demanding is the question how a Jewish movement of the 30s AD in Palestine became a union of communities throughout the Mediterranean Basin by the 80s AD. These communities were predominantly made up of Gentiles, who, at Israel's best moments, were understood to be allowed only a secondary participation in the people of God. Can what Paul have said years before Luke wrote be true, that now there is "no Jew or Gentile, but all are one in Christ" (Gal 3, 28)? How one is to explain this historical development and fix Theophilus' role in this movement is a fundamental goal of Luke.

Luke's introduction, to gospel and Acts, puts in place the plan of God, which begins with God's speaking about the marvel who was John and ends with the statement that Paul continued to teach anyone who would listen about the kingdom of God and the things of Jesus Christ (Acts of the Apostles 28, 30-31)—a conclusion to Luke-Acts, but no conclusion to the preaching to "anyone who would listen"! Jesus fits into this plan as do many others. But Jesus is the principal character of the story, and merits the title of savior. It is in his name only (Acts 4, 12) that a person will be saved. But Jesus' time on earth is only a part of the plan of God which, as Simeon noted, extends salvation to all the nations, and is brought to fruition through the missionary efforts of people who never personally met Jesus or knew his country. Acts will record in particular two events which occurred outside the gospel and which help to reveal the plan of God for salvation: Pentecost (Acts 2) and the decision that Gentile believers can be saved without practicing the corpus of law the source of which is Moses (Acts 15, together with Acts 10 – 11, 18). Anyone today who knows the basic tenets of Christianity can attest to the crucial importance these two events have played in defining a follower of Christ. Luke's gospel is not enough to explain all this. Luke's gospel with Acts is.

Second, while John the Baptist and Mary are clearly delineated in the introduction, it is Jesus in all his richness who is impressed on the reader, for, as Paul said to a wider world and some twenty years after Jesus' ascension, "it is in his name that we have been baptized, it is only he who has died for us" (1 Corinthians 1, 13). When people tried to guess who the adult Jesus was many suggestions were made, since various parts of his life suggested various renowned figures of Israel's past and of her future hopes. But the identity most profound for Jesus is best expressed, as far as Luke is concerned, by "Son of God", a son who is the product of no male procreative act, but whose conception was the result of an action upon Mary of the Holy Spirit and the power of the Most High. It is with this understanding of Jesus that Luke wants Theophilus to view Jesus' central role in Luke's story, for it is this understanding which is to define Jesus in whatever place or situation he will be found in the body of the gospel, and in the Acts of the Apostles. Certainly, Jesus will show himself to be a son in the sense of one who is obedient to a father; this he will do throughout his life, and obedience characterizes his entry into death. But underlying this active obedience is his essential make-up: Jesus is essentially divine Son of God. With this definition of Jesus in place, Luke feels ready to present to Theophilus the marvelous, mysterious and contested life (and death and resurrection) of Jesus of Nazareth. Guided by these two per-ceptions, the divine plan of salvation for all people and the divinity of the savior upon whom one calls for salvation, Luke hopes to establish for his readers a more thorough comprehension of the things his readers have been taught.

Luke's Introduction in Context

John the Baptist

The gospel of Luke follows its major source, Mark, overall but especially in the early stories of Jesus' mission in Galilee. Thus, we find in Luke the opening stories that deal with John the Baptist: John is never ignored when one is to speak about the in-breaking of God into the world in Jesus. As expected, John acts as the introduction pictured him: a preacher to bring the people to repent before it is too late. New, however, is his pointing to the "One who is greater than I", to Jesus, who will, in his own way, preach repentance. One of the most notable points of Luke's description of John's preaching is John's emphasis on fairness, justice and charity. John certainly must have known of other aspects of the Mosaic Laws and its traditions, but Luke prefers to present just his teaching about respect for others. With this emphasis Luke distinguishes himself from Matthew, Luke and John who give a different understanding of John. Luke's view of John's preaching reflects God's own actions which Mary remembers in her Magnificat and the divine choice to be born humble, poor and servant.

The Baptism and Temptations of Jesus

After the account of John's preaching we find the stories from tradition that recount Jesus' baptism in which Jesus understands, from the descent of the Spirit upon him, his mission and is called "beloved", i.e., "obedient", by God. There follow the temptations in the desert in which Jesus expresses his life's loyalty to and trust in God and his conviction that obedience to his Father's word would bring him eternal life. These last two stories make clear the interior attitudes of Jesus which explain his life and will ultimately bring him obediently to death. We recall that in the introduction we saw the child Jesus' determination to be in "the affairs of his Father", to be in "his Father's house". The adult Jesus reflects Jesus' enduring intention above all else to obey.

The Beginning of the Public Life

Once we move to the public life of Jesus we note the first major gospel section which runs from a summary description of the preaching Jesus, past his lengthy discussion with people of his village of Nazareth (4, 16-31) to his decision to "set his face" from Galilee toward Jerusalem (9, 51).

In his presentation of Jesus in the synagogue of Nazareth Luke gives what is called a programmatic story. Here are the steps in the program: 1) Jesus reveals who he is in the language of the Old Testament, i.e., the fulfillment of Isaiah's words about God's willingness to forgive sins through him (the "year" of God's pleasure); 2) the initial welcome of Jesus by his people; 3) the abrupt introduction of opposition to Jesus; 4) the prophecy that God will, as in the times of Elijah and Elisha, punish Israel "for not accepting its prophet", with the suggestion that "this prophet will be accepted only elsewhere"; 5) the attempt to destroy Jesus by violent death; the restoration of Jesus by passing through death to resurrection from the dead. This story is an account which serves as a preparation for the entire life of the adult Jesus now to follow in the gospel. With this summary of the life of Jesus to guide the reader, Luke moves on to describe, often in terms very similar to Mark's, the wonders and wisdom of Jesus. It is now Jesus, not angels or prophets, who identifies himself, and he does it by citing Isaiah (61, 1-2; 58, 6). Luke indicates that this identification does not replace but is added to what has already been revealed about Jesus in the introduction, and be the right interpretation of Jesus' baptismal experience. An important element of Jesus' self-revelation here begins a theme his preaching carries through all his life, and indeed through Acts: "Moses, the Law, the prophets all spoke about me". Finally, there is a hint in the fourth step of the programmatic story that will be full-blown in the entire Acts of the Apostles: Jesus will be accepted, if not by his own, then by many Gentiles.

A Small Insertion

Luke assiduously follows Mark's earliest stories about Jesus' miracles and teachings; they all keep alive Jesus' wise sayings, his uniqueness and his immense power and authority. But after some chapters there is a limited insertion on Luke's part, 7, 1 – 8, 3, which deviates from Mark. Wonderful stories are given in this "insertion". We have here the pity of Jesus for the poor widow, now without income because husband and son are now dead; his compassion leads him to raise the widow's son from the dead. We hear Jesus identified as the "the One who is to come", for does not his care for the sick, the lame, the blind, the poor prove that he is the Messiah? We hear of the forgiveness of the sinful woman and the criticism of the Pharisee who misinterprets the woman and Jesus. And we read the brief reference to the helpful women who, contrary to all custom laid down for the conduct of women, follow Jesus and his twelve, supporting them with their own resources.

The Messiah of God

All of this material is in service of Jesus' identity as Messiah of Israel and her savior and lord (as the angel described him to the shepherds). Thus Peter, as in Mark, identifies Jesus as the wise, powerful and holy Messiah. And, as in Mark, the potential for mystery remains: how is it that this Messiah will die crucified? In Luke's introduction we have been warned that Jesus will be a sign which will be contradicted, over whom many will "rise and fall", whose Mother will have her heart pierced because of his suffering (2, 34-36).

The Journey to Jerusalem

Once Jesus has drawn from Peter the answer to the question, "Who do you say I am?" it is time for Jesus to move to Jerusalem. It was there that Jesus spoke his only words of the introduction. Luke signals this move in a solemn way (9, 51): Jesus "sets his face" towards Jerusalem. ("Setting one's face" is a Jewish expression used to show the determination of an individual, particularly in the face of suffering.) For Luke, this journey to Jerusalem is to be seen as a part of a broad movement which extends from Galilee to Jerusalem to the right hand of the Father. It is in the light of this glorious ascension to the right hand of the Father that one is to understand, according to Luke, what will happen to Jesus in Jerusalem. Jesus is going, not simply to die, but to return to his Father through death and resurrection. Only with the time of his ascension upon him, his "being taken up", does he move to face his fate in Jerusalem. It is in the context of his own imminent suffering and death that Luke inserts Jesus' words about the disciple's possible life of suffering for him and about the future salvation of the world.

Glory and Wisdom

If the early material is mostly Marcan which leads up to the central question, "Who am I?", the section now extending from 9, 51 to 18, 14 offers little or no material from Mark, nor material shared with Matthew: Luke has other sources from which he now draws these many chapters of Jesus' public life. If earlier chapters had shown that Jesus was the promised Messiah about whom the introduction had spoken, so these chapters reveal ever more fully the wisdom of this Messiah. So profound is this teaching (most of Jesus' insightful parables appear in this section) that one is forced to see, as its source, a divine person speaking. His divinity is confirmed again by the act of transfiguration, by which one catches a glimpse of the eternal glory of Jesus before he is to look so inglorious on the cross.

The Period of Suffering
From 18, 14 Luke will again follow Mark rather closely, to arrive finally at his version of the last hours of Jesus, even to burial, and a resurrection story which closes out his gospel. As with his source Mark, Luke emphasizes the manner in which Jesus will remain with his disciples, even after death: "take and eat", "take and drink". It is in this mysterious form that he pre-eminently remains with his friends. In particular in these final hours we are not to forget Jesus' self-description as son of man, one who will be glorified and be made judge of the world after his suffering. Nor are we to forget his implied claim that he is the suffering servant of Isaiah who, though innocent, will die so that the guilty may go free. But Luke goes beyond both Mark and Matthew by highlighting Pilate's triple legal declaration: "I find no cause in this man". One can find other meanings in the tragic appearances before Pilate and the Sanhedrin and Herod Antipas, but Luke wants to show, as no one else has, that, legally speaking, Jesus was three times declared innocent. Legally speaking, his death should not have happened!

Again, we cannot but strive to understand ever more fully that the key revelations of the introduction, e.g., Jesus as Son of God, Lord, Messiah, redeemer, must be integrated with that Jesus who must die so ignominiously. Peter's confession, that Jesus is the Messiah of God, can only be understood properly in the light of this integration. We have been told from the beginning of the gospel that Luke wants to show Theophilus the plan of God, which integrates many separate events fit into a purposeful program for the good of Theophilus. Again, we note Luke's guiding hand in his preferring to report a centurion who calls Jesus "innocent" to using Mark's term "Son of God". In this way, Luke clearly emphasizes the injustice done to Jesus, an injustice recognized by anyone who is not preju-

diced against Jesus. In agreement with the centurion are those Jews, reported by Luke alone, who repent once they see the final result of their
call to Pilate for Jesus' death. Unique to Luke is the picture of the merciful, faithful Jesus, who assures the repentant thief that he will be "this day
with me in paradise", who asks forgiveness for his crucifiers, and who
commends his spirit into the hands of his Father.

Luke's Stories about the Risen Jesus

Luke presents three stories about the risen Jesus. All three have three
powerful components to show, again, that Jesus is Messiah and Son of
Man. First, there is the insistence that what had just happened in the "halls
of Sanhedrin and Roman injustice" and at Calvary was "necessary", i.e., it
was part of the plan of God, and no surprise to Him. Second, one would
have been ready for this injustice against the Messiah of God and for the
resurrection itself if one had understood that "all the Scriptures had already told you of all these things about me". Third, whether we read the
story of the empty tomb, or that of the two disciples going to Emmaus in
despair, or that of the appearance of Jesus in the upper room, we cannot
ignore the fact that no disciple believes that Jesus has risen from the dead.
They all need proof, but it will be proof which then qualifies them as
trustworthy witnesses that Jesus is indeed risen. Notable is the middle
story. In this story is played out an exchange between Jesus and two disciples that highlights "how our hearts are on fire when we hear the Old
Testament explain the events we have just experienced" and how joyful
we are "at the breaking of the bread". This story gives firm support to
Theophilus and his community to continue the practice of the Eucharist, a
blend of scripture readings and of communion with the Lord which
Luke's readers experienced each week.

A Preparation for the Acts of the Apostles

A strong force in the final of three resurrection stories is a look through
Jesus' new revelation to the mission which will be described in Luke's
ensuing Acts of the Apostles. Luke indicates in his final gospel chapter
that, if death and glorification were necessities dictated by the will of his
Father, so too the witnessing about Jesus to all nations is also a necessary
part of that divine will. The story of the life of Jesus on earth may be finished, but the plan of God continues, a plan that had been revealed at the

announcement of the future conception of John the Baptist and which continues beyond the burial of Jesus, for as Simeon had promised, some-day Jesus will be "a light of revelation to the Gentiles" (2, 32).

As Jesus had said about himself in Luke's introduction, "I must be about my Father's business" (2, 49), so now, having carried out his Father's will in his own public life, he will be about his Father's business as guide and director of his Father's world-wide program of witnessing, which characterizes his Father's offer to the Gentiles.

At this point it would be useful to provide a summary or conclusion to show the relationship of the public life of Jesus to the gospel's introduction. However, lest we obscure the close relationship between Acts and the gospel, we will give a summary only after we look at the Acts of the Apostles. For it is only in reading the two books together that one has the fullest sense of what it means to say that, with Luke, we are introduced to the saving plan of God for all people, a theme first and strongly indicated in the gospel's introduction.

The Acts of the Apostles

The Acts of the Apostles is a second volume designed to show clearly that God had a "saving plan" and that this plan was being executed throughout the known world, even to the Rome of 61-63 AD and to Theophilus. The Acts of the Apostles tells a number of stories, with new characters as the book moves on, and with plentiful change of geography and chronology. What unites all of Acts of the Apostles is given at the very beginning of the book. In one way or another all Acts carries out this directive of Jesus,

> Once you have received power
> from the Holy Spirit's coming upon you,
> you are to be my witnesses
> in Jerusalem,
> throughout Judea and Samaria,
> and to the ends of the earth. (1, 8)

"You will be my witnesses" carries a double sense throughout Acts: "my witnesses" means both "witnesses from me" and "witnesses about me", to the ends of the earth.

These words of Jesus begin to be fulfilled in Chapter 2 with the gift of the Spirit on the Jewish feast of Pentecost; it is here that we read:

"It will come to pass in the last days", God says,
"that I will pour out a portion of my Spirit upon all flesh.
Your sons and daughters will prophesy…
Indeed, upon my servants and handmaids
I will pour out a portion of my Spirit in those days,
and they shall prophesy" (2, 17-18)

As God's words suggest, "all flesh" will receive the divine Spirit of God; thus the gift of the Spirit at this Jerusalem moment is to be understood as the first of many outpourings of the Spirit. Indeed, wherever we read of a person's choice to believe in Jesus we are to understand that the Spirit has come to dwell in that person (2, 38). At Pentecost particularly the gift of the Spirit produces in miraculous form a speaking on behalf of God (i.e., prophecy) which exalts the "wonderful acts of God" (2, 11), and, with Peter's speech, gives the first answer to the question "what is the meaning" of this Pentecost.

Once the Spirit is given in Jerusalem we find believers, particularly the twelve, who are strong and wise witnesses through this gift of the divine Spirit. We read of various types of witness to Jesus in Jerusalem in Chapters 2–7. We have further witness to Jesus in greater Israel in Chapters 8–12. And we have still further witness to Jesus as we leave Israel for the wider Mediterranean world, from Syria, through what is today Turkey, through Greece, to Rome, in Chapters 13–28. Witness can be varied: living the Christian life to the full (as in the case of most of those who are baptized in Acts), dying for Jesus, preaching about Jesus, whether one confronts Jew or Gentile, working miracles in the name of Jesus. When one is finished reading Acts one realizes that old names, such as Peter, such as the twelve, no longer appear. There are new names, such as Paul, Barnabas, Timothy and Silas, who are now the preachers. Indeed, we can say that Luke writes about a third generation of Christians, most of whom did not even have solid information about the Palestine so familiar in the stories of Luke's gospel.

Theophilus

Theophilus, the recipient of the Gospel, remains the recipient of the Acts of the Apostles (Acts of the Apostles 1, 1). It is through the two volumes together that Theophilus will better comprehend the reliability of the truths he has been taught, particularly how God's salvation came to him. The beginnings of Christianity, evidenced in Luke's gospel infancy stories, strongly suggest a divine plan to save Israel: how is it that a Gentile such as Theophilus has full membership in a movement that was originally all-Jewish?

The Role of the Gentiles in the Mystery of Christ

We should be clear about the importance of this divine plan for Gentiles. We admit that Jewish religion in the first century AD allowed for the presence of Gentiles within itself. These people, unlike the pagan Gentile, worshipped the true God and kept His Law and, to the degree possible, contributed financial support to the Jewish religion. They were a "part" of the people of God. Still, one had to face the fact that the benefits promised by God to Abraham were promised to "Abraham and his descendants". When "descendants" was interpreted as meaning physical descendants there remained the nagging doubt as to whether one not physically born from Abraham could share fully in the glorious benefits promised by God. Gentiles could and did participate in the Jewish religion, but, it was arguable whether the Gentiles were inheritors of the Kingdom of God. At the end of Luke's gospel and Acts there is no doubt that both believing Jew and believing Gentile could be equal sharers of that "mystery" which has Jesus for its foundation and Lord. As St. Paul's famous formula about the believers in Christ has it, "There is no room any more for distinction between Greek (i.e., Gentile) and Jew, between circumcised and uncircumcised" (Colossians 3, 11).

Jew and Gentile in the Mystery That Is Jesus

In the book of Acts Jesus, the light for salvation to the Gentiles, is preached to Jews particularly in the first seven chapters, but also in almost all of the following two chapters and in many chapters thereafter as well. Indeed, though the story of God's plan eventually moves from Palestine to the broad pagan world, preaching always reaches Jews according to the plan "to the Jew first, then to the Gentile". With Chapter 10 Luke presents a powerful, indeed a key story for Acts: the story about Peter and Cornelius, which sets the direction for much of what follows to the end of the book. Cornelius, a pious follower of the Lord, believes in Jesus through the testimony of Peter. God's gift of His Spirit to Cornelius demonstrates the pleasure of God in this Gentile, and Peter, at first hesitant, finally and without full understanding moves to offer baptism to one who has faith in Jesus. The implications of the pagan's faith in Jesus are spelled out in Chapter 15 when Peter, referring to his experience with Cornelius, formalizes the argument as to why a Gentile Christian need not keep the Law of Moses for his salvation. If requires that one who has put his faith in Jesus is pleasing to God, is purified and gifted with the Spirit of God, then Cornelius and every other believing Jew and Gentile is saved without living the Jewish way to salvation revealed by God to Moses. God asks obedience to Jesus, not to Moses. Thereafter Luke brings his reader through a series of testimonials to Jesus in a variety of communities, always concentrating on both Jews and Gentiles, even in Rome. The clear implication is that the Gentile believer is now not a peripheral part of the people of Israel, but belongs with Jews as a full participant in the mystery which has only faith in Jesus as its foundation.

Given the linear structure and the parallel succession of testimonies, worth citing again is the famous phrase of St. Paul whose influence is clearly present in Luke's presentation. Paul had said often, especially as regards his own missions and testimony, that God wanted the word to be preached "first to the Jew, then to the Gentile" (Romans 1, 16). Acts follows this directive, as one moves from Jerusalem, through the rest of Palestine, to present-day Turkey, then Greece and finally Rome. Like Paul, Luke respects the plan of God for Jew and Gentile by having preaching directed first to the Jew and then to the Gentile.

The Holy Spirit in Acts and the Introduction

As one thinks of these apostles and of all the witnesses in the lengthy story of Acts, one asks oneself how they became such determined and clever preachers and witnesses of faith in Jesus. Luke recounts the crucial story for Acts and for the plan of God: the Feast of Pentecost. In Acts of the Apostles 2, the group of Jesus' followers, about 120 persons, are gathered in prayer in the upper room. At the chosen moment, God pours out His own Spirit upon these people; the result is the rush to tell every one who had come to their house of the "wonderful things of God".

The Pentecost event reveals the Trinitarian aspect of the divinity; the divine Holy Spirit of God is poured out by the Father through the hands of the Son of God, Jesus (Acts of the Apostles 2, 33). This reality reflects Jesus' own promise to his disciples at the end of the Gospel: "Wait here in Jerusalem for the Gift of My Father". Since Pentecost is the true beginning of the witnessing activity which will reach Rome in 61-63 AD, the Spirit continues to be the energy and intelligence that speaks through all the witnesses of Jesus in Acts. Even a statistic such as the fact that the Spirit appears more than fifty times in the twenty-eight chapters of the book is indicative of the Spirit's enduring presence among the disciples. One inevitably asks where else have we seen such a forceful and enduring act of the Spirit. The answer comes in three moments in the gospel.

The first moment is in the promise that John the Baptist will have the Holy Spirit from his birth. We hear no more of the activity of the Spirit in John, but we can suppose it is found in the holy life, preaching and announcement of Jesus.

The second moment is implied in what was reported in the annunciation to Mary: that Jesus is conceived through the power of the Holy Spirit (1, 35). Whatever else can be said about Jesus, whatever titles he may be given later on, it is this remarkable, indeed unheard of description of his conception that plumbs most profoundly the deepest meaning of Jesus of Nazareth. Thus, wherever we meet Jesus, in gospel or Acts, it is a Jesus who is radical product of the Holy Spirit of God. Jesus, in all situations, is divine. From the initial action of the Spirit upon Mary one gathers that the Spirit of God is at the very beginning of God's new intervention into human lives and continues in the effect of his action upon Mary, and this intervention is Jesus.

The third moment occurs after Jesus has been baptized by John; Jesus is alone, in prayer, when he receives the Holy Spirit. From that moment on, Jesus' entire life changes and he becomes the powerful and wise Messiah of Israel. The cause of this life-directing moment is the Spirit—yet again the Spirit. All that follows of Jesus' public life is a time in which the Spirit empowers Jesus to live and work as he did.

Thus, from his infancy and throughout his public life, Jesus is the focal point of the very Spirit of God. The Spirit has a significant place from the beginning of what we have determined to be the central issue of Luke-Acts: the demonstration of the saving plan of God for all peoples.

But what underlines the Pentecost in this plan of God is that, whereas in Jesus' life, he is the only one to receive the Spirit of God, now, with this generous sharing of His Spirit, all believers receive the Spirit of God. Thus, within the continuity of the divine plan, there is a new gift to mankind: now the Spirit is given, not just to Jesus, but to all believers.

Jesus and the Spirit in Acts

But the Pentecost story tells us something else that is important to know in order to comprehend what Luke wishes to convey. That is, whereas the prophet Joel had made clear that "God would pour out His Spirit", Peter makes clear that it is Jesus who poured out the Spirit: "Exalted to (or by means of) the right hand of God, Jesus received the promise of the Holy Spirit from his Father and then poured forth that Spirit" (2, 33). Thus, whereas people in Acts will be empowered by the Spirit to give heroic witness to Jesus, as Jesus was empowered in the gospel, it is Jesus who, in Acts, gives the Spirit. Jesus is central to the plan of God, not only as the one in whom one is to have faith, whether in Jerusalem or in Rome, but also as the one who directs the mission through his constant gift of the Spirit. Paul earlier had distinguished the abiding presence of the Spirit in the believer and the gifts of the Spirit, given in various ways and degrees to many of the earliest Christians; Luke does not make this distinction, but concentrates on the power of the Spirit for witness, with occasional and important references to the Spirit whom the baptized will receive (2, 38). The Spirit, then, is a major force in Acts as in the gospel; the Spirit joins with Jesus, who asks for witness from Paul: "The God of our ancestors designated you to know His will, to see the righteous one and to hear his voice...to witness before all to what you have seen and will see and hear" (Acts of the Apostles 22, 14-16).

As Jesus, then, under the influence of the divine Spirit, preached that the Kingdom was near and called for faith in himself, so now Jesus' disciples, under the influence of the same Spirit at the direction of Jesus, call for faith in Jesus who will come again.

Ways of Witnessing to Jesus

A point worth making in discussing Acts is that witness to Jesus as the light for the salvation of the Gentiles is not only the witness found in preaching. Granted that the speeches of Acts are major instances of witnesses which often move people to belief in Jesus and are key points of book (notice the rhythmic spacing of the major speeches: Chapters 2, 3, 7, 10, 13, 15, 17, 20, 22, 26), yet there are other kinds of witness that deserve our attention.

Witness through Christian Life

Early in Acts we meet those who listened to the Pentecost witness of Peter and the apostles, repented, were baptized in the name of Jesus Christ for the forgiveness of their sins, and then received the Holy Spirit (Acts of the Apostles 2, 38). Acts describes these Jewish Christians in terms which suggest religious perfection among Jews: they devoted themselves to the teachings of the apostles and to the communal life, to the breaking of the bread and the prayers (Acts of the Apostles 2, 42-43). These people are further described as sharing their possessions so that no one among them was poor (2, 45; 3, 34). Thus, not all witnessing consisted of preaching; note the impression made by these Christians on those around them: "The people esteemed them highly" (5, 13). This communal witness consisted of living out the commandments: you shall love the Lord God with all your hearts...and you shall love your neighbor as yourself. Nowhere else, neither in Old nor New Testament, not even in the rest of Acts, do we find a community of such witness to the ideals of Christianity.

Witness through Spiritual Gifts

Another type of witness in Acts is the frequent meeting with people who have received special gifts of the Spirit. These gifts, notably prophecy and speaking in tongues, are intrusions into ordinary human life which cannot but astound listeners and make Christian beliefs credible. Apart from the followers of Christ at Pentecost, many Christians in Acts, the most famous of whom are Barnabas and Paul, enjoyed these gifts to benefit their communities.

Witness through Suffering

A third kind of witness in Acts is that of suffering and martyrdom for one's faith in Jesus. Peter represents the earliest community; almost from the start of his preaching, he faces accusations and imprisonment (cf. Chapter 12 of Acts). Strife in Jerusalem culminates in the violent death of Stephen, a deacon, and the subsequent fleeing from persecution in Jerusalem. Paul also is to face many forms of opposition and, indeed, he was told about this in his inaugural vision (9, 16). Luke singles out Peter and Paul, but it is clear that others, often their companions, are forced to suffer, too. A fourth of the book of Acts presents Christian life under the cloud of opposition to Christian preaching. Perhaps Jews are the most opposed to the preaching about Jesus as Savior and completion of the Old Testament, but Roman officials, for whom religious subjects are usually of minimal interest unless they threaten Roman peace, are not beyond imprisoning and beating Christian witnesses.

Direct Witness by God

Acts does record a further type of witness, one not ordinarily grouped with the testimony of preaching, Christian life, spiritual gifts and suffering for one's faith. This is the witness of God Himself, of Jesus, of the Spirit. The most impressive of these acts of witness in Acts is the divine intervention of Jesus in Paul's plans, which were certainly plans of good faith and zeal. Paul wanted to enter Asia, a province of what is now present-day Turkey, only to have the Holy Spirit tell him not to go there (16, 6). Similarly, when Paul reached Bithynia, another part of today's Turkey, the Spirit of Jesus would not allow him to enter that territory (16, 7). Well known is the intervention of the Holy Spirit and of angels in the event we know as the conversion of Cornelius. Neither Peter nor Cornelius understood all that was happening to them; only God understood, and He alone moved them to play out their roles. Jesus himself is responsible for much of what Paul preaches; as he notes in calling Paul to be his preacher, "God has chosen you...to see the Just One and hear his own voice speaking, because you are to be his witness, testifying to what you have seen and will see and hear" (22, 14-15; cf. 26, 16). Not easily forgotten are the words of Jesus to Paul, when Paul was about to flee from his persecutors: "Be fearless; speak out and do not keep silence: I am with you. I have so many people that belong to me in this city (Corinth) that no one will attempt to hurt you" (18, 9-10). God, then, in many instances enters into human history to enable His witnesses, with fortitude and with proper words, to execute the divine plan for salvation—thereby God becomes a witness to Himself.

Paul's Speech at Athens

One of the most unexpected witnesses on behalf of Jesus of Nazareth is Paul's speech to the Athenians (17, 21-32). In this situation Paul must address his message to "pure" pagans. Astonishingly, he speaks of Jesus only once, in his very last sentence. He does not mention Jesus' name, but only the judicial function of "a man raised from the dead" (32). All the rest of the speech is a witness to God and to the pagan efforts to finding the true God. This speech reminds us that, though the disciples are to witness to Jesus (1, 8), their complete witness is to God, to the One who crafted the divine plan of salvation of all peoples, at the center of which plan God put Jesus. How varied indeed was the witness of the early Church to the societies it encountered in the divine offer of salvation to all!

Finally, we should mention the wonders God performs at various stages of the witness to Jesus. These wondrous acts show to Theophilus God's message of salvation inexorably reaches Theophilus through God's almighty power. God's continual miraculous efforts throughout the first-century history of the Church reveal a God who protects, encourages and, before all else, loves. God is determined to work with the witnesses to Jesus in order to bring salvation to all. To this end, God continues to offer Jesus as the one whose name one calls on for salvation. This is in perfect harmony with the gospel introduction which identified Jesus as the Savior who is Christ the Lord. In his Pentecost speech Peter had noted that God commended Jesus to Israel by working signs and wonders and miracles through Jesus (2, 22). He continues these astounding actions so as to provide singular witness to Jesus and to the divine plan.

Conclusion

Acts, then, is written to illustrate, through a variety of experiences, the overall witness to Jesus that reached Theophilus and thus explain the origins and content of his faith. As noted, Jesus is recorded as the source to execute God's plan, the source of this Christian movement from Jerusalem to Rome, so that Acts is a perfect complement to Luke's gospel. Each of the two works is a part of the story of God's intervention to save mankind through the efforts of Jesus of Nazareth. One detects in both gospel and Acts the same atmosphere: there is a calm and a peace and a resolve and an assurance that characterizes both books. This atmosphere is most evident in the infancy narratives of the gospel. Even in this way of writing the introduction of Luke prepares the reader for the continual effort of the author to present all that happens as the unstoppable plan of God. It is a divine plan that Acts presents to Theophilus; as such, neither book is intelligible by itself without the reader's knowledge of the whole. Though Acts makes clear the value and importance of the Jesus experience to the ends of the earth, it can never substitute for the wealth of this experience in the gospel—just as one could never grasp the energy and devotion and fulfillment experienced in the period of Acts through reading the gospel alone.

Summary

Each evangelist has his purpose in writing. This purpose is in great part determined by what the authors see as the needs of their audiences and determines what stories they will use to attain their goals. To help him achieve this purpose he has introduced the public life of Jesus (for Luke we include Acts) with an original and perceptive introduction to the meaning of Jesus, a meaning not always drawn by people from Jesus' public life.

Mark's audience was suffering for its faith in the region of Rome. A highly suspect minority which did not support Roman religion, Mark's Christians had to understand two things. First, they should never lose sight of the power, wisdom and holiness of the Jesus to whom they had committed themselves. Within this picture of Jesus the audience must try to understand the divine plan according to which their beloved Messiah Jesus must die so horribly. Second, they must understand that to be a disciple of this Jesus one must follow him even if, as in the case of Jesus, that involves death for one's belief. To give the disciple encouragement, we see a Jesus who is himself faithful to his Father to the end. The Father remains faithful to Jesus through the end, to life eternal. To achieve his goal, Mark introduces his story as a story about Jesus, Messiah and Son of God. That is, Jesus, believed to be Messiah, is such even in death in obedience to God; Jesus, believed to be divine Son of God, will live his life and his death in complete obedience to his Father. The few words of Mark's introduction, "Jesus, Messiah and Son of God", direct our attention to his purpose in writing: to encourage Christians to remain firm in belief and to obey as did the divine Son of God.

One cannot fail to see that John's gospel concentrates on the person of Jesus as the only one who can give life. The Johannine gospel depends heavily on knowledge of Judaism. One is not surprised at this for it is a gospel of Jewish Christians responding to the accusations of Jews that they are believing in a false Messiah. Indeed, one senses that the smoldering antipathy between Jesus and his opponents is a literary indication of the antipathy existing now, 65 years later, between the Jewish Christian community and its Jewish opponents. To the Jewish-Christian minority

John directs a profound study, by means of his introduction, of the one in whose name they have been baptized. For John to know Jesus is to know much more than that he is Messiah, the hoped-for king who will provide all the good blessings of God's kingdom. Jesus is the union of the Word with human flesh, the Word who was "in the beginning, with God and indeed God", who was the cause of all that exists, who is life and light, and, above all, Son of the Father. Thanks to this introduction John has furnished us not with a teaching about moral life, but with a deep understanding of Him who will give us life even though we die. Gospel miracles and speeches, then Jesus' death, if perceived correctly, argue strongly that the believer in Jesus will live without end.

Matthew's audience is the latest of a line of Jewish believers in Jesus who have had to suffer for their belief. Those who opposed them were Jewish, too. They were the Jews who felt obliged to reject Jesus as their Messiah and eliminate his memory. Matthew comes to the aid of his audience, a minority against a majority, with a story which argues strongly that Jesus, and only Jesus, qualifies to be Messiah of Israel. He has no equal in Jewish history, and is the fulfillment of all its prophecies of hope. Moreover, Matthew capitalizes on his audience's faith that Jesus is divine. Obviously, to be Son of God is incomparably unique and a major support for the belief that the kingdom of God will come through Jesus as Messiah. To achieve his goal, Matthew presents two chapters of introduction. One of the striking points of this introduction is the fulfillment of the Old Testament in Jesus. Even the genealogy of Jesus shows how he and his "going to all nations" is the result of his ancestry. Another major point of the introduction is the divine certitude that stands behind the belief that Jesus is born of a virgin, through the power of the Holy Spirit of God. His name fits his adult role perfectly, "through him God saves". But he also deserves, as Isaiah suggests, to be called "God-with-us", an aspect of Jesus not easily grasped from his public life alone. Finally, with the visit of the Magi and subsequent events, one senses that Jesus will suffer for being who he is. This intuition that comes to realization on Calvary. At the same time, through the Magi, Matthew alludes to the future adoration of Jesus by Gentiles, adoration in which the Jewish opponents of the Christian community will participate one day. Jesus is Messiah and Lord of Israel. With this rich introduction Matthew can strengthen those Jewish Christians who face strong opposition from their fellow Jews.

Luke's gospel and Acts of the Apostles have a particular goal in mind: to help Theophilus understand how reliable are the things he had been taught. Prominent among these things is the comprehension of the new attempt by God to save all people. In this way Theophilus is led to understand why the message, first preached to the Jews, is now preached to the Gentiles, to himself and his community. Luke unites Theophilus' awareness of his Christianity to the historical figure of Jesus through an exposition of the saving plan of God. This exposition emphasizes the divinely-attested certitude of the relevance of all the events and teachings. Luke tells his stories with emphasis on this divinely-attested certitude. One can feel secure in one's belief in Jesus. God is the guarantor of this account of salvation, whether it be the account of the conception of John the Baptist or the account of the arrival of Paul some sixty-five years later in Rome, or the account of any matter in between.

The plan of God and His saving hand can be traced in every event. Jesus reminds his Jewish disciples that "all the Scriptures spoke of me", but for Luke the person of Jesus is to be placed within the great plan of God. Since God wants to save all peoples, Jesus will be as savior and "Lord of all", as Peter tells the gentile Cornelius. Jesus is clearly revealed in the infancy stories as Son of God, Lord and Messiah, light of the nations and glory of Israel. But given that Luke wants to show Theophilus how certain was the act of salvation which reached him and his community, Jesus, divine Son of God, is savior in an altogether special way: "Everyone who calls on his name", Luke says, "will be saved". The energizing and unifying act which spans all the years and experiences from Jesus to Theophilus is baptism in the name of Jesus Christ (Acts 2, 38).

There can be no doubt from the way Luke presents his materials that God is the one who brought Jesus and Theophilus together. In this way Theophilus understands himself as loved by God (as his name indicates) and redeemed by one who is worthy to be called Messiah, Lord, and, most of all, Son of God. To help Theophilus gain this assurance about the things he had been taught, Luke feels he needs a second volume in which witnesses from and about Jesus will bring God's offer of salvation, first to Jews, then to all peoples. Pentecost and the Cornelius story stand out as major historical events of a salvation which was first offered to Israel and now fills the world with blessings of the Holy Spirit of God. Everyone who repented and believed in Jesus Christ received the one and same

Spirit of God (Acts of the Apostles 2, 38). In both the gospel and Acts Jesus is savior, pointing to a divine plan of God which Jesus and the Spirit of Jesus execute with Jesus at its center. The introduction of the gospel is the clearest expression of the plan which, the reader of Luke-Acts senses, explains God's continual offer of salvation. This gospel introduction gives ultimate meaning to the life of Jesus and the experiences of Christians which culminate in the experiences of Theophilus and his community.

* * * * *

In case of each gospel, the story of the adult, public life and death of Jesus is best understood by paying close attention to the introduction and how each of the evangelists presents it in accord with the particular needs of his audience. It is through the introductions that we particularly appreciate the wonder of Jesus Christ, the revelation of God, through whom we learn of the love that brought Him to offer salvation to all.

STAMPA: Febbraio 2009

presso la tipografia
"Giovanni Olivieri" di E. Montefoschi
ROMA • info@tipografiaolivieri.it